YORK FILM NOTES

Taxi Driver

Director
Martin Scorsese

Note by Pete Fraser

Longman

York Press
322 Old Brompton Road, London SW5 9JH

Pearson Education Limited
Edinburgh Gate, Harlow, Essex CM20 2JE, United Kingdom
Associated companies, branches and representatives throughout
the world

Stills courtesy of Columbia Pictures. Taxi Driver written by Paul Schrader
Printed by Courtesy of Columbia Pictures

First published 2000

ISBN 0-582-40506-8

Designed by Vicki Pacey
Phototypeset by Gem Graphics, Trenance, Mawgan Porth, Cornwall
Colour reproduction and film output by Spectrum Colour
Printed in Malaysia, KVP

contents

author of this note Pete Fraser is Head of Media Studies at Long Road Sixth Form College, Cambridge and a Principal Examiner of A level Media Studies. He has a degree in Film and Literature from the University of Warwick and an MA from London University Institute of Education in Film and Television Studies for Education. He has contributed to a number of publications including *Watching Media Learning* (Buckingham ed., Falmer Press, Basingstoke, 1990).

TAXI DRIVER **y**

background

trailer

Out of a cloud of steam, hissing and spuming from a manhole, the snout of a New York taxi emerges. This is the first image of Martin Scorsese's *Taxi Driver* and right away you know where you are. Dante had a word for it. The New York taxicab, filthy, rattling and jouncing over the cratered streets, is alienation on wheels, a perfect image for the city as inferno ... a disturbing, frightening film, it has the desperate excitement that goes with its vision of the city.

Jack Kroll, Newsweek, 1 March 1976

In its own way, this movie, too, has an erotic aura. There is practically no sex in it, but no sex can be as disturbing as sex. And that's what it's about: the absence of sex, bottled-up, impacted energy and emotion, with a blood-splattering release. The fact that we experience Travis's need for an explosion viscerally, and that the explosion itself has the quality of consummation, makes *Taxi Driver* one of the few truly modern horror films.

Pauline Kael, The New Yorker, 9 February 1976

Utilising Bernard Hermann's most menacing score since *Psycho*, Scorsese has set about recreating the landscape of the city in a way that constitutes a truly original and gothic canvas ... the final upsurge of violence is less cathartic than lavatorial. The nauseating effluence of the giant flesh emporium that the film has so single-mindedly depicted.

David Pirie, Time Out, reprinted in Milne, 1982, p. 587

Taxi Driver is about the inner disgust of the male psyche ... a man who's so fed up with filth and the misfortunes of living in a big

trailer

one of the most critically acclaimed films of the 1970s

city, that he's about to take his own life, and several others, in his hands.

Michael Lieberman, internet movie database, www.imdb.com

The grimy underside of New York (but it could just as easily be Sydney or London) is gutted and exposed for us to explore through Travis's jaundiced eyes. His impetuous actions take us with him on a seamy ride through his meagre life as though we are in the back seat of his cab. After twenty-three years, this movie still stands as a monument to the fine art of cinema.

Flint, internet movie database, www.imdb.com

reading taxi driver

One of the most critically acclaimed films of the 1970s, regularly voted into 'all-time Top 100' lists, *Taxi Driver* was the film which cemented Martin Scorsese's credentials as the most important director of the new Hollywood. The first of four collaborations between Scorsese and writer Paul Schrader, the film features a virtuoso performance by Robert De Niro as the taxi driving anti-hero, Travis Bickle. It won the prestigious *Palme d'Or* for Best Film at the Cannes Film Festival in 1976 and was nominated for four Oscars (Best Picture, Best Actor for Robert De Niro, Best Music for Bernard Herrmann's score and Best Supporting Actor for Jodie Foster).

With interiors shot in a condemned building and location work in New York, the film mixes techniques of documentary realism with some expressionistic camerawork, including lots of slow motion, to evoke the dreamlike state of Travis's mind. Though Schrader's original screenplay is in the main closely followed throughout, Scorsese's improvisational technique comes to the fore quite frequently. The running order of scenes is changed slightly in the final film, though the original plot remains intact.

Hard-hitting themes, explicit use of strong language and particularly the violence of the final sequences may come as a surprise to some audiences, perhaps used to the assumption that contemporary films are more 'extreme' than those of a quarter of a century ago. The bloody finale to the film almost led to it being given an 'X' certificate in the USA, which could have limited its audience, but with changes in post-production it was granted an 'R', which meant that viewers under 17 could see the film with a parent.

A cross between a gothic horror in a modern setting, a film noir and John Ford's western, *The Searchers* (1956), *Taxi Driver* draws upon a vast range of influences from both cinema and literature (see Contexts: Genre and Influence) whilst still being wholly original. It comes from a period of filmmaking between the death of the Hollywood studio system and the arrival of the blockbuster, when a new generation of film directors were able to make highly personal and often very original films.

The period in which *Taxi Driver* was made was a traumatic one in American history. Despite the symbolism of the moon landings in the late 1960s and early 1970s, which re-asserted America's position as the leading nation on Earth, there were many problems both at home and abroad. The assassinations of the Kennedy brothers and of Martin Luther King were shocking events. The challenges to the racism at the heart of American society in the form of both the Civil Rights movement and more militant groups such as the Black Panthers reminded the country of just how bad life could be for many of its citizens. The corruption revealed by the Watergate scandal of 1973, in which President Nixon eventually had to resign after admitting he had lied to the people and tried to undermine the democratic process, made many lose faith in their leaders.

Perhaps more than any of these domestic traumas, the Vietnam War (1961–73) led to many Americans questioning their whole system of values; it became difficult for them to understand why young men were being sent to fight and often die in a war in the Far East, particularly when American television news began showing pictures of atrocities committed in the name of the USA. Mass protests by opponents of the war hastened its ending, but for others it was felt as a a humiliating climbdown. Subsequently, many who returned from fighting in Vietnam found it impossible to re-adjust to life back home.

This period of social and political change is reflected in the cinema of the time, which often exhibits both the energy of those who were looking a cult classic

to transform American society, but also the anguish of those who had suffered.

Taxi Driver, which touches upon several of the areas described above, has become a cult classic, with internet sites devoted to it and references from it appearing in a range of cultural artefacts. Travis's mohawk haircut has been copied many times and the line 'You talkin' to me?', from one of the most memorable scenes in the film, quoted as often as any line from cinema.

key players' biographies

MARTIN SCORSESE

Director Martin Scorsese was born in 1942, in New York City. The son of Italian American Catholic parents, he grew up an asthmatic youngster in the Little Italy area of the city. Due to his medical condition, he was unable to play out with other kids much, so he tended to spend a great deal of time in movie theatres, or watching films on TV and working on storyboards and comic strip film ideas. Originally he saw himself as material for the priesthood, but dropped out of religious college after a year and entered New York University, where he obtained his masters degree in film and studied for nearly a decade.

Many of his films reflect his upbringing and cultural background. They also often refer to his film viewing experience, with moments in them borrowed from films he saw as a child from a diverse range of genres and directors. His first feature film was *Who's That Knocking at my Door?* (1969), starring a young Harvey Keitel. Scorsese went on to make *Mean Streets* with Keitel and De Niro in 1973, both films being set in the environment where he had grown up. He made *Boxcar Bertha* for low-budget producer Roger Corman in 1972 and again featured Keitel in *Alice Doesn't Live Here Anymore* (1974) in which Jodie Foster also appeared.

Scorsese was excited by the script of *Taxi Driver* which he first read in 1972, but needed the success of *Mean Streets* to justify being given the resources to make the film. His third film with De Niro, *New York, New York* (1977) was a commercial failure, but it was followed by a film frequently voted the

Martin Scorsese and
Robert De Niro discuss
a scene from Taxi Driver

best film of the 1980s, *Raging Bull* (1980), made in black and white and based upon the life of the boxer, Jake LaMotta. His next film, another study of maniacal behaviour, *The King of Comedy* (1982) also starred De Niro. Scorsese had earlier developed a second strand to his career with three documentaries, *Italianamerican* (1975), based around his family, *American Boy* (1977) about Steven Prince, who plays Andy the gun seller in *Taxi Driver*, and *The Last Waltz* (1978) a carefully structured concert film celebration of rock group 'The Band'.

Scorsese returned to a low-budget project with a dark comedy set in New York, *After Hours* (1985) but followed this with his biggest production to date, *The Color of Money* (1986) starring Tom Cruise and Paul Newman, the latter reprising a role from *The Hustler* (1961). Scorsese's next project was the highly controversial *The Last Temptation of Christ* (1988) which was picketed by religious protestors on its opening and accused of blasphemy.

By the 1990s, Scorsese had become acclaimed as the greatest living American director, particularly after his gangster epic *Goodfellas* (1990), where he once again teamed up with De Niro. The following year he had a hit thriller with a remake of *Cape Fear* (1991), again starring De Niro, this time as a psychotic ex-convict taking revenge on a lawyer and his family. Scorsese made a surprise foray into the costume drama genre with an adaptation of the Edith Wharton novel *The Age of Innocence* (1993) before a return to the gangster milieu in *Casino* (1995, again featuring De Niro). In 1997 his subject matter was another religious leader, the Dalai Lama in *Kundun*, set in Tibet. Most recently, Scorsese has returned to the New York setting with a darkly humorous film about a paramedic having hallucinations, *Bringing Out the Dead* (1999), which is his fourth collaboration with Paul Schrader (see Filmography).

Scorsese is renowned for his exciting visual style, both in the mise-en-scène and the camerawork. Thematically his films are dominated by studies of edgy individuals, religion and violence. He is also a champion of cinema and its history, always talking in interviews of the range of influences upon his own work from his vast viewing experience. This is epitomised in his narration/ presentation of the three hour film *A Personal Journey through American Movies* (1995).

written during a bout of depression

PAUL SCHRADER

Born in 1946, screenwriter Paul Schrader's strict Calvinist upbringing meant that he was not allowed to see a film until he was eighteen. He made up for lost time as a student at Columbia University, New York and on UCLA's graduate film programme. His influences were European directors, such as Robert Bresson from France and Carl-Theodor Dreyer from Denmark, and the Japanese filmmaker Yasujiro Ozu. His dissertation, *Transcendental Style in Film*, which examined the work of these three directors was later published and he had a spell as a film critic. He began writing screenplays, hitting the jackpot for *The Yakuza*, when he was paid the then-record sum of $325,000. *Taxi Driver* was written in the early 1970s during a bout of depression; the success of the film allowed Schrader to start directing his own films.

In an interview with Mark Cousins for the BBC's *Scene by Scene* series, Schrader described the genesis of the screenplay:

> It was written as self-therapy in a dire period of my life. A number of things had gone wrong, I was drifting, I had pain in my stomach, a bleeding ulcer; I hadn't spoken to anyone in weeks ... I was like a person in an iron coffin, surrounded by people but absolutely alone. I wrote that script so that I wouldn't become that character.
>
> *Schrader, Scene by Scene, 1998*

The closeness of the writer to the character has been explored by Peter Biskind in his behind-the-scenes exposé of 1970s filmmaking *Easy Riders, Raging Bulls* (1998). Biskind describes an occasion where screenwriter John Milius took Schrader to a sporting goods shop in Beverly Hills in search of a pistol:

> The clerk showed him a .38 that felt good in his hand, cold and hard. He saw a girl over by the tennis racquets, sighted down the barrel at her head, and tracked her around the store as she moved, clicking the trigger a few times. 'If there ever was a psycho you shouldn't sell a gun to, Paul was it', said Milius. 'I told this story to Scorsese and he put it in *Taxi Driver*.'
>
> *Biskind, 1998, p. 286*

biographies background

Scorsese requested Herrmann as composer

Schrader has collaborated with Scorsese as screenwriter on three other films, *Raging Bull* (1980), *The Last Temptation of Christ* (1988) and *Bringing Out the Dead* (1999). His other screenplays include: *Obsession* (1976), *The Mosquito Coast* (1986) and *City Hall* (1996). He has written and directed *Blue Collar* (1978), *Hardcore* (1979), *American Gigolo* (1980), *Mishima: A Life in Four Chapters* (1985), *Light Sleeper* (1991), *Touch* (1997), *Affliction* (1997) and *Forever Mine* (1999). He also directed *Cat People* (1982) and *Patty Hearst* (1988).

MICHAEL CHAPMAN

Michael Chapman, the cinematographer of *Taxi Driver*, began his career working on *The Last Detail* (1973). He has been Director of Photography on more than 30 films, including: *Invasion of the Body Snatchers* (1978), *Dead Men Don't Wear Plaid* (1982), *The Lost Boys* (1987), *Ghostbusters II* (1989), *Kindergarten Cop* (1990) *The Fugitive* (1993) and *Space Jam* (1996), as well as working with Schrader on *Hardcore* (1979) and with Schrader, De Niro and Scorsese on *Raging Bull* (1980).

BERNARD HERRMANN

Bernard Herrmann, born in 1911, wrote the music for *Taxi Driver*. He started his musical career early, winning a composition prize at the age of thirteen and founding his own orchestra at twenty. After writing scores for Orson Welles's radio shows in the 1930s (including the notorious 1938 *War of the Worlds* broadcast), Herrmann moved on to film scores with *Citizen Kane* (1941) for Welles, later becoming a prolific film composer, producing his most memorable work for Alfred Hitchcock, for whom he wrote nine scores, including the haunting melodies of *Vertigo* (1958) and the shrieking violins of *Psycho* (1960).

Scorsese requested Herrmann as composer partly because of watching a four hour double bill of Truffaut's *The Bride Wore Black* (1968) and Hitchcock's *Marnie* (1963), both of which were scored by Herrmann. He wanted a sense of menace and madness but also the rhapsodic theme, 'more to do with the internal person, the New York feeling'. Herrmann's music gives a sense of being rather like a vortex, never quite coming to completion; Scorsese wanted this feeling in order to provide what he

Herrmann changed his mind on reading the script

described as 'the psychic basis ... the music that supports or even carries the image' for this 'New York gothic' film:

> I begged and pleaded until he eventually agreed to do the film because he was my first and only choice. You get to know what you like if you see enough films, and I thought his music would create the perfect atmosphere for *Taxi Driver*. I know I was right, Travis Bickle was the kind of person who didn't listen to anything besides the voices in his own head, and I was convinced the only person who could capture this state of mind was Bernard Herrmann.
>
> *Martin Scorsese, sleevenotes for the soundtrack CD*

When Herrmann was first approached, he simply said 'I don't do films about cab drivers' but when he looked at the script, he changed his mind, since Travis was very much the kind of obsessive character that Herrmann's music for Hitchcock had been built around. It was the first time Scorsese had worked with a composer for his films, as previously he had used a rock soundtrack to emphasise character emotions.

Taxi Driver was to be Herrmann's last score and, extraordinarily, he died just hours after recording it with an orchestra, on Christmas Eve 1975. The final shot of the film is a dedication to his memory.

ROBERT DE NIRO

Born in 1943, Robert De Niro trained as a method actor. He had previously appeared in Scorsese's *Mean Streets* as the volatile Johnny Boy, (in some ways a model for the darker Travis, with his idiotic grin and volatile near-psychotic behaviour). He later collaborated with the director on *New York, New York, Raging Bull, King of Comedy, GoodFellas, Cape Fear* and *Casino*. In many ways, his screen persona has often been used as Scorsese's alter ego.

De Niro is known to be obsessively attentive to detail for the roles that he plays. For his part in *Taxi Driver* he lost 15lbs and researched the life of a cabbie by working as one for a number of weeks. He also interviewed and tape recorded some people from the Midwest in order to learn the accent

'method' involves improvisation

for the part. Later for *Raging Bull*, he put on 60lbs to play Jake LaMotta in later life after learning how to box to gain authenticity for the fight scenes. For *New York, New York*, he learned all the saxophone movements for his character.

The 'method' involves a strong element of improvisation and there are many points in *Taxi Driver* where De Niro used this. A comparison of the dialogue in the screenplay with the scenes in the finished film reveal a number of such instances. In scenes with Cybill Shepherd, Jodie Foster and Harvey Keitel, much of the dialogue can be credited to De Niro. Foster has described how, for their breakfast scene, he made her go over the dialogue again and again until she was both completely comfortable and also bored with it; then suddenly he would throw in improvisations. Having polished the improvisations, the actors would then be ready to shoot the scene.

De Niro also had an image in his mind of the character of Travis as a crab:

> walking sideways with a gawky, awkward movement. Crabs are very straightforward, but straightforward to them is going to the left and the right. They turn sideways, that's the way they were built

Brottman, 1999, p. 51

He perfected a walk for Travis which echoed this. It is particularly noticeable in the scene where he shoots the raider in the shop.

His partnership with Scorsese has produced some of his most memorable roles but he has also worked with a number of other top directors including Francis Coppola, Bernardo Bertollucci, Brian DePalma and Sergio Leone. In 1974, De Niro received an Academy Award for Best Supporting Actor for his role in *The Godfather: Part II*, and later received Academy Award nominations for Best Actor in *Taxi Driver, The Deer Hunter* (1978) and *Cape Fear*. He won the Best Actor award in 1980 for *Raging Bull*. He has moved into the role of producer himself heading his own production company, Tribeca Film Center in the 1990s, and directed *A Bronx Tale* in 1993.

Academy Award nomination

As one of Hollywood's most bankable names, he has been much in demand for both starring roles and cameo appearances for a quarter of a century. In recent years he has been less obsessive about preparation for his film roles, partly because he now does three films a year rather than an average of one. This has also meant more of a supporting role at times, such as in *Jackie Brown* (1997) rather than carrying the whole film as a star vehicle.

HARVEY KEITEL

Harvey Keitel, born in 1939, who plays the pimp, Sport, was originally earmarked for the part of the campaign worker, but persuaded Scorsese to give him the part of the pimp, which he then worked on to develop. He has worked with Scorsese on a number of occasions, namely in *Who's That Knocking at my Door?*, *Mean Streets*, *Alice Doesn't Live Here Anymore*, *Taxi Driver* and *The Last Temptation of Christ* as Judas. He has carved out a long career for himself particularly as a cop and as a gangster type. He first came to prominence in the early films of Scorsese after working in theatre for a decade. His career was rejuvenated in the early 1990s with appearances in *Thelma and Louise* (1991), *Reservoir Dogs* (1992), *Bad Lieutenant* (1992) and *The Piano* (1993), illustrating his diversity as an actor.

CYBILL SHEPHERD

Cybill Shepherd, born in 1950, did not originally want the part of Betsy, seeing it as too limited. She had previously appeared in four films, including *The Last Picture Show* (1971) and *Daisy Miller* (1974). She later became much better known for her two long-running TV series, as Maddie opposite Bruce Willis in *Moonlighting* and as Cybill Sheridan in *Cybill*.

JODIE FOSTER

Jodie Foster, born 1962, who plays the teenage prostitute, Iris, started her career at the age of two, appearing in commercials. After various TV and film roles, *Taxi Driver* was her real breakthrough, gaining her an Academy Award nomination for Best Supporting Actress. Though she never took acting lessons, she was the first actress to receive two Oscars before the

Foster's career started at two years of age

Jodie Foster as Iris

Foster had to undergo psychiatric tests

age of thirty, firstly for her part as Sarah Tobias in *The Accused* (1988) and then for her performance as Clarice Starling in *Silence of the Lambs* (1991).

The character Foster plays was based upon a teenage prostitute who Schrader had met in research for the film (who appears in the film as Iris's friend). As Foster was only thirteen at the time the film was made, she had to undergo psychiatric tests to check that she would not be adversely affected by the role. Her twenty-year-old sister was used as a **body double** for her.

Now one of Hollywood's most bankable female stars, she has also moved into directing with *Little Man Tate* (1991) and *Home for the Holidays* (1995). Other notable films in which she has appeared include: *Bugsy Malone* (1976), *Foxes* (1980), *Sommersby* (1993), *Contact* (1997) and *Anna and the King* (1999).

authorship

Unlike a novel or a painting, which can be seen as the creative endeavour of one individual writer or artist, a film is the result of the creative input of a lot of people, each of whom could be seen as putting his or her own 'stamp' upon it. The screenwriter may come up with the original idea and expand it on paper, as with Paul Schrader for *Taxi Driver*, which came at least partly from his own experiences. The actors may bring the characters to life even down to creating ideas for how they should look, as Harvey Keitel did with his wig and hat, or for what they should say, as various actors, notably De Niro and Peter Boyle did with their polished improvisations. The cinematographer has the job of putting together the 'look' of the film and the composer will contribute a considerable amount to the atmosphere and potential emotional impact of the film with the score. The **editor** has to make choices about how the footage will be put together to make sense for the audience. But in overall creative charge of the film is the director, who will control the artistic decision-making process.

Like the conductor of an orchestra, it is the role of the director to get the most out of all the individuals working together to create the whole piece.

a collaborative medium

The director must have an overall vision for the film and may indeed have the single controlling vision, but ultimately is in charge of what is a collaborative project.

In western culture, individual authorship tends to have high status and value attached to it; we talk of the plays of Shakespeare, the novels of Jane Austen, the paintings of Van Gogh; in each case it is the personal vision of the artist which is valued and even revered. Sometimes this can carry monetary value with it too, as in the extraordinary prices paid for paintings by famous artists. In other areas of our lives, a form of authorship could even be seen to carry value in such things as designer labels (such as Versace) or even brand names (like Nike), which can sell for much higher prices than high street chains.

For a collaborative medium such as film, the notion of authorship is obviously more problematic than with individualistic art forms. Early film critics, trying to promote cinema as an art form tended to assume that only in places where the individual filmmaker had a lot of creative freedom and control over their projects could he or she be seen as the author of the film. Thus filmmakers like the Russian director Sergei Eisenstein or the Swede Ingmar Bergman, who tended to have a lot of freedom in contexts where profit was not the key factor, were valued the most.

By contrast such critics saw Hollywood, dominated by the pursuit of profit and a production line atmosphere, where projects were simply assigned to whoever was available, producing 'popular entertainment', but nothing of value in terms of an 'art' form.

The French critics from *Cahiers du Cinema*, a publication begun in the 1940s, were the first to suggest that maybe individual authorship could be assigned to Hollywood films too. They argued that the individual stamp of a director could transcend the system and even the factory-line products assigned to him (and in the period of the studio system it almost always was 'him'). They sought in the apparently 'cloned' genre films of the system some individualistic traits which marked one film out from another and carried the stamp of an auteur. Thus they began to value the work of a number of directors, Howard Hawks, Alfred Hitchcock and John Ford among them. In each case they looked for thematic concerns which produced a thread running through a number of films by the director, even across genres which on the surface were quite different. They also looked for repeated motifs across formal aspects, such as the use of camera or mise-en-scène. Hence the obsession with mother figures and the influence of the past on the present in Hitchcock's films could be taken alongside Hitchcock's editing style as evidence of his personal stamp or vision.

Ultimately, this seeking out of an author was designed to make films respectable objects of study; on the whole, at the time it had little impact on the way in which films were sold or indeed on audience choices, which were still more determined by star and genre. However, the new wave of filmmakers in the 1970s did tend to get marked out as having their own distinctive styles and thematic concerns, so that in Scorsese's films, a very distinct set of thematic concerns and stylistic motifs may be identified. Notable amongst these would be his treatment of the city, his Catholicism, his deconstruction of masculinity, his use of the colour red and of a nervous shifting camera, all features evident in *Taxi Driver*.

AUTHORSHIP TODAY

More recently, the director as auteur has increasingly become a selling point for films, particularly with the work of directors like Tarantino. The director as star, with lengthy interviews about his or her work will often be used as a marketing device particularly for niche audiences. While perhaps only Spielberg is a household name on a par with Disney as a selling point for films, a name like Scorsese will be known to sufficiently wide an audience to generate interest in any of his projects. Perhaps too with more media coverage of cinema and the rise of film study as a more mainstream educational activity there is a greater expectation of cineliteracy on the part of the audience.

There is also a sense in which the auteurs themselves come out of a different tradition to their Hollywood predecessors. Where under the studio system it was, in effect, an apprenticeship that led to learning the craft, in more recent years, filmmakers have emerged from film school as 'cineastes' first and foremost themselves.

authorship background

AUTHORSHIP AND TAXI DRIVER

Part of this search for authorial voice has tended to be a search for authenticity of experience, somehow reflected in the film itself. For *Taxi Driver*, the screenplay is clearly reflective of an actual period in Schrader's life and he, Scorsese and De Niro all said that they could understand how the character of Travis felt:

> When I read Paul's script, I realized that was exactly the way I felt, that we all have those feelings, so this was a way of embracing and admitting them, while saying I wasn't happy about them ... It was a way of exorcising those feelings
>
> *Scorsese, 1989, p. 61–2*

In a visual sense, the film has connections with the director's autobiography:

> the whole film is very much based on the impressions I have of growing up in New York and living in the city. There's a shot where the camera is mounted on the hood of the taxi and it drives past the sign 'Fascination', which is just down from my office. It's that idea of being fascinated, of this avenging angel floating through the streets of the city, that represents all cities for me
>
> *Scorsese, 1989, p. 54*

In *Taxi Driver* there are additional dimensions to authorial debate as two auteurs worked on the project and thus it can be seen as an intersection of each of their thematic and stylistic concerns. For Schrader, the Calvinist upbringing, city as inferno and personal depression is linked with for Scorsese the myth of the city and a Catholic sense of guilt. This intersection perhaps provides some of the most provocative material and perhaps explains some of the contradictory impulses of the film's presentation of Travis.

Robin Wood has explored this territory:

> [Scorsese's] films operate within a liberal humanist tradition whose boundaries and limitations remain only hazily defined ... Paul

> Schrader's work, on the other hand, can be quite simply characterized as quasi-Fascist ... Although some clash of artistic personalities and ideologies lies at the heart of *Taxi Driver*, I do not see any possibility, even were it desirable, of sorting through the film to assign individual praise and blame.
>
> *Wood, 1986, p. 51*

Wood sees *Taxi Driver* as a flawed film partly because its ending is unresolved and a coherent message for the spectator is not possible to discern from it. In essence he blames this on the contradictory creative inputs of Schrader and Scorsese. We shall return to this later, to look at how the two men themselves offer very different explanations of their intentions with the ending. However, Wood's view does raise the question with which we began this section: where does authorship lie in a film?

The many influences upon the creators themselves (filmic, literary, even news stories), the input of the actors (improvisation, but also what meanings they carry as stars from the other roles that they have played) and even the distinctive use of music (with its highly emotional charge) are all key factors in how we might interpret the film. Furthermore, there is an even wider sense in which collective authorship might be applied to the film. Some critics have drawn attention to the way in which the New York of *Taxi Driver* is almost like the New York of the audience's imagination, so that perhaps authorship needs to be seen as a collaboration not just amongst the film's makers, but also with its audience too. What the audience brings to the film intersects with what was put there by the filmmakers to create meaning.

narrative & form

For the purpose of this detailed analysis, the film will be broken into segments or sequences along the pattern of the chapters in the recent DVD release *Taxi Driver: Collector's Edition*. For each sequence, the events will be outlined (action) and then some of the significant features of cinematography, mise-en-scène, editing, soundtrack, character, narrative and themes will be indicated (commentary). Where a point in the commentary refers to another sequence, this is followed by the chapter reference of the sequence in brackets. Films mentioned in this section appear in the Filmography.

Quotations from the dialogue are from the film unless specifically stated as being from the published screenplay.

1. start

ACTION

The title sequence begins with a yellow cab emerging through swirling pink smoke. The driver's eyes are shown in close-up, moving slowly from side to side. The cab appears to glide through the lights and the rain of night time in the city as the main credits play. The soundtrack introduces the main themes of Bernard Herrmann's score. As the smoke clears, there is a dissolve in slow motion into the next scene, Travis arriving at the company office.

foreshadows the bloody ending

COMMENTARY

The first thing to appear after the Columbia pictures logo is Robert De Niro's name in blood red; his role as the star of the film is thus established but there is also the first foreshadowing of the bloody ending of the film which is echoed at various points in the film's colour scheme. The smoke is indicative of the New York environment, being a typical feature of the city, but it also serves an expressionist function, suggesting at the very least impending danger and to some critics the fires of hell.

Shot in slow motion, a device which will be used a lot in the film to suggest the strangeness of Travis's existence, an almost nightmarish state, the shot continues with the emergence of a yellow cab looming through the smoke, dragging the film's title behind it, written in yellow which echoes the colour of the taxi itself. The music builds, an ominous theme with heavy pounding drums and low notes. The rest of the principal cast and crew names appear in yellow as the cab drives.

Then as the music turns to the jazzier romantic theme on sax and piano, we see close-ups of Travis's eyes, shifting from side to side as if watching everything in the city around him, a prowling detective-avenger. Again, this prefigures what is to come, as much of the film will centre upon his obsessive looking at others. For the audience too, as we are uncomfortably drawn into his world, the act of looking at him and sharing what he sees may be a disquieting experience.

These shots in the cab have echoes of a number of films which Scorsese remembers seeing when he was younger. In his BBC interview with Mark Cousins, he refers to De Niro's eyes here being reminiscent of those of Robert Helpmann in *Tales of Hoffmann* (1951). Indeed, he used the same technique as filmmakers Michael Powell and Emeric Pressburger used there of running the camera at 36 or 48 frames per second instead of 24 to give the eerie slow quality (sending the film through the camera at faster speed makes the action look slower, and vice versa). The shots through the cab windscreen as the wipers go back and forth in the rain echo the opening of another Powell and Pressburger film, *The Small Back Room* (1948), where passers-by are also indistinctly seen.

The driving sequence in *Psycho* (1960) – another complex study of puzzling psychopathology – just before Marion reaches the motel as the wipers go back and forth in the rain, is similarly referred to here. It is also possible to discern the influence of Michael Powell's highly disturbing study of a serial killer, *Peeping Tom* (1960), of which Scorsese championed the 1979 re-release, where again the audience is drawn into a sympathetic relationship with someone performing repugnant acts. In the opening shots of *Peeping Tom* we see an enormous close up of the killer's eye and are drawn into a seedy world of the city at night, obsessive looking, violence and prostitution.

As the car glides through the rain and the smoke it is both an extension of the central character, a mysterious outsider, and a recognisable symbol of New York itself. It will serve as his means of transportation around the city, the vehicle by which he will gain his impressions of the city and its inhabitants and will also be his means of introduction to some of the key characters in the film.

An active construction of point of view is effected right from the outset of the film. There is a sense in which Travis is helpless to avert his eyes from what he sees in the city, but there is also a sense in which what he sees is all pretty horrible. The spectator is made to gaze with Travis, to see the world as he sees it. This is done through the appearance of the people in the street, and whenever he drives in his cab. Prostitutes and gangs are on every street corner; likewise prostitutes, their clients and potential murderers are his fares.

As Robert Philip Kolker puts it:

> Neither coincidence nor a reflection of 'reality' explains why the only people Travis sees are the mad and the disenfranchised, ... why the cafeteria frequented late at night by him and his cronies is populated only by pimps and nodding drug addicts. These are the only people and the only places of which Travis is aware. They constitute the only things he perceives, and, since the viewer's perceptions in the film are so restricted to his own, the only things the viewer is permitted to perceive as well.
>
> *Kolker, 1988, pp. 192–3*

2. travis bickle

This is the only sequence in the whole film to be out of chronological order, since in the next scene Travis goes for his job interview, so this driving must appear later in temporal terms as he is already driving the cab here.

2. travis bickle

ACTION

Travis is introduced in the cab company office, applying for a job. The audience learns of his inability to sleep at night and his desire to get a job which will enable him to work long hours. He is willing to work in any part of the city. His interviewer (the Dispatcher) asks him about his military record and Travis reveals that he had an honourable discharge from the marines in Vietnam.

Accepted for the job, a typical night is shown as he drives through the city, picking up a prostitute and her client. Travis's thoughts are played as he writes his diary talking about a typical night and his contempt for the city. In the morning, he walks out of the cab depot and goes into a porno cinema. He has an embarrassing exchange with the concession girl, asking her name, and then goes into the cinema where he is shown watching the (out of focus) film.

Back in his apartment on the bed, Travis's diary entry continues with his description of Betsy who he first sees outside the campaign office. She is shown in slow motion described as 'like an angel'.

COMMENTARY

This series of introductory scenes tell us a lot about Travis and his lifestyle as well as indicating the start of four key strands of the narrative: he gets the job driving the cab, he desires to clean up the streets ('Someday a *real* rain will come'), he first sees Betsy (the object of desire) and the posters are first shown for the candidate Palantine's campaign which will lead to Travis's aborted assassination attempt.

The sequence begins with a static image (as does every sequence in the film), in this case of the Dispatcher sitting at his desk reading his paper. In slow motion, the smoke clears as Travis enters the door and the music continues from the opening. Again this smoke is clearly used expressionistically and not diegetically. It is not smoke in the cab office, but a hangover from the city streets which follows Travis around and makes a visual point about him being separated from other characters, who are not trailed by smoke in this way despite working the same city.

As Travis enters the cab office, his name is visible on the back of his combat jacket (Bickle T). The jacket itself is a khaki hue, reminiscent of the military and contains on the sleeve a logo of 'King Kong Company' itself a reference to a famous movie monster who comes to New York. This jacket is precisely described in Schrader's original screenplay and as with the boots Travis wears, apparently belonged to Schrader himself, perhaps underlining the autobiographical nature of the story. The name Travis denotes travelling, a character who is restless and wandering, while Bickle has a hard and unpleasant edge to it, like 'bickering'.

As the music fades and the slow motion ends, there is a cut to an over-the-shoulder shot of the Dispatcher. Above him framed in a window are two drivers apparently arguing and to his right is a sign with a set of big instructions to drivers, particularly focusing on what has to be done in the event of accidents. One of the two drivers framed in the window is a character later introduced as Wizard, though in this sequence he is wearing a cap which makes him unrecognisable as the bald driver we later meet. Throughout the conversation between Travis and the Dispatcher there is a very long held shot of Travis (24 seconds), grinning inanely whilst standing as if he is still a member of the armed forces rather than an interviewee for a driving job, who might be expected to be seated in such a situation. Travis is unshaven, reinforcing his restless lack of sleep and lack of attention to his own appearance. He sports a check shirt and boots, perhaps a reference to his midwest/cowboy origins, as well as his combat jacket.

The interchange between Travis and the Dispatcher is echoed by the argument framed in the window above the desk as the dispatcher tells Travis off for his lame joke about his driving licence, 'Clean. As clean as my conscience' with 'Are you tryin' to bust my chops?'. Travis's military background is established, giving him a link to the Dispatcher, who also

overhead shot

served in the marines. It also serves as a possible explanation for Travis's psychological trauma and inability to fit in. An honourable discharge suggests mental scars rather than physical invalided him out of the war and ties the character into a tradition of post-Vietnam war films such as *Born on the Fourth of July* (1990). It is referred to only obliquely later in the film in terms of Travis's own regime being reminiscent of military training and his commando-style assault at the end of the film. Unlike in some other post-Vietnam war films, the soldier's wartime experiences are not used in *Taxi Driver* as the sole explanantion of his entire psyche.

Travis's disconnectedness is emphasised in his inability to understand slang terms as he asks 'what's moonlighting?', not surprising given his explanation of his education 'some, here, there ...'. It is also emphasised by the way he is framed separately from other characters. The scene ends with one of the overhead shots which recur throughout the film and will most spectacularly emerge in the shooting sequence with the slow-motion tracking shot which surveys the carnage. The shot here is of the desk as the Dispatcher hands the forms to Travis. Later it will be repeated several times, so that something is set up at a subliminal level for the audience, foreshadowing its final use in the film.

As Travis goes out into the main cab parking area, the character later introduced as Wizard leaves at the same time but walks in a different direction. Here there is one of a number of very distinctive uses of the camera which break with the continuity system and appear unmotivated by the action. Taking in the 'Slow Down!' and 'Stop!' exhortations on signs, which might be seen as directly addressed to Travis in view of his later actions, the camera leaves Travis and does a 360 degree pan around the garage, beginning by apparently following Wizard. This kind of shot apparently caused consternation amongst the crew, since it went against the continuity editing with which they had grown up.

It is a good example of Scorsese's distinctive stamp upon the film's stylistic system as well as something of a homage to the work of the French New Wave, a shot used by Truffaut in *The 400 Blows* (1959). Again the colour red is prominent as a reddish glow is exuded by the garage as the camera pans around it.

2. travis bickle

a life of mass consumption

Outside, Travis walks down the street in the sunshine and in another break with editing convention, the shot dissolves as he swigs a drink. Usually, such an edit would signify the passing of time, but here it is used for the passing of no more than a few seconds. The edit is used again in the film, both when Travis destroys the TV set (chapter 19) and in the final sequences (chapter 27) as the camera leaves the scene of carnage. It also appears in a later Scorsese film *After Hours* (1985), where it is used as the central character goes up some stairs. As with the 360 degree pan and the slow motion, the device is as much about emphasising the dislocated nature of the character of Travis, since he isn't even shot or edited 'normally'.

In the next part of the sequence, Travis's voice is heard as he writes his diary in his apartment whilst visually the audience is introduced further to his world. This storytelling device was taken by Schrader from Robert Bresson's *Diary of a Country Priest* (1950) and also from Dostoevsky's novel *Notes from the Underground* (1864). It presents the audience with a characters point of view on both a verbal and a visual level and since he is writing in a diary his voice on the soundtrack is motivated by the action, rather than being a non-diegetic voice-over. The camera presents a first glimpse of his apartment, stark, bare and scruffy, beer cans hanging from the wall, a coke can crushed and another on his desk next to an empty quarter pounder box. Travis's life is one of mass consumption existing on junk food, popping pills, watching daytime soaps on TV and porn films at the cinema. The mirror in which Travis is just visible as the camera pans around will be important later as Travis performs his ritual preparation (chapter 15). The bars on the window reinforce his sense of entrapment.

His haphazard diary is scrawled in pencil in an exercise book. Driving slowly, Travis passes judgment on the people of the city:

```
all the animals come out at night; whores, buggers,
skunk pussies, fairies, dopers, junkies ... sick,
venal. Someday a real rain will come and wash away
all the scum.
```

Thus his comments are visualised for us by the images of passers-by in the city, but we also know these are the words he was writing in his room, so they overlap from the previous shots. At this point we see the rain-soaked streets, but as Travis uses the word 'rain', clearly it also refers to his actions at the end of the film and perhaps to some kind of vengeful God-figure who will wash away sin.

As the cab travels through the city, the camera is at a low angle, passing a cinema showing one of the most notorious and influential horror films of the period, *Texas Chainsaw Massacre* (1974), supported by *Return of the Dragon* (1972), a martial arts film. Both could be seen to refer to Travis himself: the first representing the carnage of the final scene (chapter 27), the second his ascetic training for it.

The amusement arcade he passes named 'Fascination' perhaps more than anything sums up the contradictory nature of the city – repellent, what Robin Wood (1986) describes as 'the excremental city' (p. 51) – yet also something to which both Travis and the audience is almost magnetically attracted. This contradiction is also echoed in the music as, from time to time, the ominous theme changes to the jazzy love theme throughout the film.

Several of the shots in this sequence are close-ups of aspects of the car. The wing mirror and the rear view mirrors, which provide much of the detail of Travis's observations of city life, the badge on the car which marks Travis out like the Sheriff of a western, investing himself with authority. Travis's point of view is offered as we observe street life, mini-skirted prostitutes, passers-by, the neon of the city.

These close-ups are characteristic of the fragmented way in which Travis will view the world throughout, never quite grasping the bigger picture. As Mikita Brottman notes, Scorsese offers the viewer both bodily fragmentation in the camera use and psychic fragmentation in the form of the diary extracts in voice-over:

> shots of Travis's eyes in the rear view mirror, shots of the back of the head, headless torsos, torsoless heads, close-ups of arms and heads, various overhead shots of tables, counters and desks with

> hands extending over them ... a disembodied voice laying bare his
> soul to an unseen listener.
>
> *Brottman, 1999, p. 56*

The outwardly respectable white client, urging him to hurry up as he paws
the black prostitute with the grotesque blonde wig in the back of the cab
is presumably typical of such fares picked up by Travis. As he talks in his
diary about having to 'clean off the come' and even the blood from the
back seat, we see him looking disgusted as he throws away a cloth.

Travis's squalid lifestyle once the driving stops is represented by his trip to
the porno theatre first thing in the morning. As he walks to the theatre, the
audience sees the shot used on the poster for the film and later for both
the video and DVD covers. This shot is frequently seen as representing
'God's Lonely Man' and has become almost emblematic of the film.
Scorsese himself expressed his surprise at the way audiences were not put
off by the poster, with its slogan 'in every city there is one man' and that
on the contrary, it often had the opposite effect.

This sequence emphasises Travis's inability to connect with women as he
tries to chat up the concession girl with the noise of onscreen sex in the
background and the spools of the 16mm projector visibly running behind
his head. It also foreshadows the sequence later where he takes Betsy to a
porn movie (chapter 8). He acquires yet more junk food, with another of
the series of overhead shots occuring as he pays for the items, a magazine
article open on the desk entitled 'how you spend your money affects your
sex life', which itself appears to refer to Travis's inadequacy. Next to the
counter in the foreground is a statue of the Venus de Milo, a totem of high
art in a squalid environment.

As Travis goes into the tiny cinema, the camera closes in on the reflection
of the projector, with a close-up of some fingers stroking female genitalia
visible. Like the mirrors on the car this emphasises the fragmented nature
of Travis's experience and his constant role as an observer rather than
participant. Inside the cinema, a few indistinct males are visible and the
screen itself appears to be wildly out of focus, like Travis's world view.

2. travis bickle

emblem of the film

'God's lonely man' –
the image used on
the poster for Taxi Driver

documentary of the mind

Back in his apartment, the camera shows Travis on the bed, a stack of pill bottles visible to the rear standing upon a suitcase, emphasising the temporary nature of his existence. A can of coke is on the bed and newspapers are strewn around. The camera rises up almost to an overhead shot. Travis is heard as his diary continues:

```
All my life needed was a sense of some place to go.
I don't believe that one should devote his life to
morbid self-attention. I believe that someone should
become a person like other people.
```

Ironically, of course this is the opposite to what happens to Travis; he remains morbidly self-obsessed, communicating only obliquely with others and sets himself a mission which is largely inappropriate. The last thing he becomes is 'like others'.

There is a cut to documentary-style footage of the street, with a hand-held camera amongst the crowd; a street scene reminiscent of those in *Mean Streets* (1973) and a contrast to the expressionistic style shown elsewhere in the film. Some of the passers-by actually look at the camera, so much of this is verité style. Yet at the same time it is divorced from reality in that it is shot in slow motion. Yellow cabs are all around and the shot is emphasised as if a point-of-view shot. From out of this emerges the figure of Betsy, in slow motion, a technique Scorsese has described as a 'documentary of the mind' as described in Travis's diary:

```
I first saw her at Palantine Campaign Headquarters
... She was wearing a white dress. She appeared like
an angel out of this filthy mess.
```

Her first appearance is shown watched by an anonymous character played by Scorsese himself, casually seated on a ledge in the doorway as she walks into the campaign office. The dissolve which accompanies this takes us to a close-up of Travis's scrawled and childish handwriting, 'They cannot touch her'.

Travis's awkwardness is thus further emphasised, partly through his handwriting and partly through his stuttered voice-over and the audience is given the option to question his version of Betsy. This opportunity is taken further when we leave Travis outside and are witness ourselves to Betsy's everyday flirting with Tom.

He sees her as a kindred soul, but also as a virginal figure. She is dressed as an angel, moves in an ethereal way in slow motion, has long blonde hair and even has a harp playing in the background on her first appearance. In reality, however, her smouldering look is more knowing and sexualised than this angelicism suggests.

Scorsese has explained Travis's unrealistic view further:

> When Travis falls in love with a woman, he can't admit he wants to make love to her. That's forbidden. What he feels for her is like a ... fantasy of the Blessed Virgin.
>
> *interview with Guy Flatley, in Brunette, 1999, p. 55*

A row of cabs outside the Palantine office move in unison as the lights change, while the huge poster of the candidate is reminiscent of those in *Citizen Kane* (1941) when Kane stands for election with similarly empty rhetoric. The camera tilts and zooms in on the doors and the scene cuts to inside.

3. tom and betsy

ACTION

At the Palantine campaign headquarters, the audience is introduced to Tom and Betsy. The latter notices that a taxi driver has been staring at her from his cab, so Tom goes out to ask him to move on. It is Travis and he races away. At night we see him prowling around in the city without a fare, eventually picking up a middle-aged female passenger.

COMMENTARY

Tom and Betsy occupy a different kind of world to that of Travis. They are well-dressed, educated and articulate. Betsy is dressed in a yachting blazer, while Tom wears a light suit and tie. Both wear glasses, giving them an aura of intellectualism that Travis never has. Theirs is the world of politics and clever conversation, epitomised by Tom's phone call about the badges and the subtle difference between 'We are the people' and 'We *are* the people'. Albert Brooks, who plays Tom, was a stand-up comic on TV who Scorsese brought in to play the part. He was given scope to develop the role by adding to the dialogue himself.

Tom and Betsy flirt as he says 'you sound like we're selling mouthwash' and she replies, 'we are selling mouthwash', indicating the superficiality of their politicking or lack of belief in Palantine's rhetoric. The mise-en-scène of the campaign headquarters is also starkly at odds with that of Travis's enclosed environments. The big windows and the light airy open plan office signify a place of interaction and modernity.

When Tom goes out to speak to Travis, the latter immediately drives away at speed, a pre-echo of his later escapes from the Palantine rallies (chapters 14, 18 and 24).

4. wizard's court

ACTION

Travis goes to the all-night diner where the cab drivers hang out. Wizard is holding court and tells a tale of his alleged sexual exploits with a female passenger. Travis tells Dough-Boy of a story of violence he has heard on the radio, the latter offering him the chance to buy a gun.

COMMENTARY

As Travis enters the diner, he passes a poster for another candidate, the ironically named Goodwin. Travis is greeted similarly ironically as 'the ladies' man', while Wizard makes his outrageous boast. Once again, sexual energy is bubbling away beneath the surface of the film, yet there is no real sex in it. People look (at sex films), people talk (about sex), but nobody is actually seen doing it, least of all the celibate Travis.

Again Travis is shown misunderstanding slang as Dough-Boy asks him 'how's it hangin'?' He does a sort of slow doubletake on this as if assuming its sexual connotations, finally realising it means 'what's happening?'. His reply is to talk in second-hand terms about a story he has heard on the radio, a random attack by 'some crazy fucker' who cut off another driver's ear. He talks about the areas of the city where he is prepared to go and others are not; as he does so, he looks at two very ominous black characters, one with an enormous bow tie, tapping slowly on a table. As elsewhere in the film, it is clear that Travis is a racist, aligning blacks with the 'scum and the filth'.

The 'alka seltzer' shot has often been noted as one of the most odd in the film. There is a **track**in on a big close-up of Travis's face and then a reverse of this with a slow-motion track into a huge close-up of his glass. Described by Larry Gross as 'symbolic of a precipitous descent into the effervescent disturbances of Travis's inner world' (Gross, 1976, p. 44), it is also a reference to Godard's *Two or Three Things I Know About Her* (1967) where it is used on a coffee cup.

It is an example of what one of the film's editors, Tom Rolf, has described as a Scorsese technique of making a shot inordinately long and therefore making the audience look at it from a different perspective. Rather than cut a shot short, Scorsese would suggest holding it for longer so that the audience is forced to think about it having some additional purpose.

5. new volunteer

ACTION

Tom and Betsy discuss a newspaper seller with missing fingers who is nonetheless able to light a match; they are interrupted by the arrival of Travis, who says he wants to volunteer to help the campaign. He proceeds to ask Betsy to come for coffee and pie and they agree that he will return at four o'clock the same day to take her. The meeting takes place and she tells him he reminds her of some lines from a Kris Kristofferson song. She agrees to a further date, at a cinema. In the meantime, Travis goes to buy the record she mentioned, as a present for her.

COMMENTARY

The story which Tom and Betsy discuss has parallels with the shooting at the end where Travis shoots off part of the man's hand. The possibility of the man being a mafia victim also relates to the film's ending where Travis appears to have unwittingly destroyed a mafioso (chapters 26–8). This scene is part of a whole set of quirky conversations in the film, most of which involve Wizard and the other drivers.

Travis's arrival sees him dressed differently for the first time in the film. He wears a scarlet velvet jacket and light trousers, setting him apart from the Travis shown hitherto. His chat-up is still embarrassing but just about credible in his highly direct approach. Throughout the sequence Tom is hovering, usually framed between the pair of them. The familiar overhead shot appears, this time of Betsy's desk.

Later at the cafe, when Betsy tells Travis, 'I don't believe I've ever met anyone quite like you', it prefigures (as does the whole scene) the later cafe sequence with Iris, when she says 'I don't know who's weirder, you or me' (chapter 22). The two characters tend to be framed separately by the camera in the cafe, emphasising the uncloseable distance between them. Travis and Betsy are seated in front of a window with a vertical line which keeps them apart even when they are on screen together. Travis often misinterprets Betsy's words, such as the 'pusher' line from Kris Kristofferson (who he has never heard of). His joke about getting 'organezizied' falls flat; later we see he has just such a notice in his apartment and as he sees his 'destiny' he vows to become organised.

Their conversation is largely based around Travis's opinion of Tom, 'I think he's silly' and upon Travis's insistence that he sees some kind of bond between himself and Betsy. This departs considerably from the original screenplay, where Travis talks about his life as a taxi driver. (Paul Schrader *Taxi Driver* pp. 23-5.)

The framing of this sequence with Travis's voice-over serves to emphasise his point of view. His banal description of their choice of pies stands alongside his views of the city and what needs to be done about it, constantly mixing the everyday with the shocking.

6. charles palantine

ACTION

Travis picks up a fare, who turns out to be the presidential hopeful, Palantine, along with two aides. Palantine asks Travis his opinion on what needs doing for the city and gets told it in no uncertain terms, to his great unease.

COMMENTARY

The first glimpses of Palantine come in the mirrors; when he asks for Travis's opinion, he does not get a response to which he can subscribe. As in other sequences, most of this one has Travis framed separately from the other characters. He is shot mainly side on whereas we see Palantine from the front, indicating the gap between Travis and other people in terms of attitudes, behaviour as well as physical distance.

When Travis does say what he would change about the city, it is couched in terms of purgation and cleanliness. He describes the headaches he gets and the feeling of sickness, but he also talks of cleaning up the streets and flushing them down the toilet. It is this obsession with filth and cleanliness that ultimately drives his actions.

This scene precedes the first meeting with Iris (chapter 7) and follows the first meeting with Betsy (chapter 5), thus introducing three key characters in the film.

Palantine gets out of the cab at the St Regis hotel, which is where Travis picks up Betsy at the end of the film (chapter 28). In the screenplay, Tom is one of the aides in the cab, but this was changed for the film.

7. aborted fare

ACTION

Travis's first encounter with the teenage prostitue, Iris. She gets into the cab and asks Travis to drive, but is pulled out by Sport, her pimp. He tells Travis to forget what he has seen and leaves him a crumpled twenty dollar note.

COMMENTARY

Iris was chosen as a name for the character because it is so at odds with her existence. An archaic name, the name of a flower, amidst all this city 'filth'. She is dressed like an undersized hippy in her big floppy hat and hotpants. Sport, meanwhile, looks like an Apache Indian. The twenty dollar note becomes symbolic for Travis, who keeps it out of his main money box, an almost sacred object. Iris, as the 'whore', is the opposite of Betsy, the symbolic 'virgin', but she is also similar to her in Travis's eyes, the innocent child sullied by the city, a symbolic princess to be rescued.

Travis is offered the role of rescuer but he fails to act in this instance, sitting motionless in his cab, only his eyes moving as he looks in the mirror at Iris. This same motionlessness occurs in the sequence later (chapter 10) where the backseat passenger talks about shooting his wife. It is only outside the taxi that Travis later starts to take action, with devastating results.

As Sport pulls Iris from the cab, we are given a side view which frames them both only at crotch level. We do not get a clear view of either Foster or Keitel's faces, though as an audience we probably recognise them both from their voices. Sport's admonition to her, 'bitch be cool' is a contrast to the later dancing scene where he describes her as 'my woman' (chapter 23).

As Travis drives off, his cab is attacked by a gang of black youths; this is part of a whole series of incidents involving black characters which see them appear in a negative light, reinforcing Travis's racist ideology (chapters 4, 10, 11, 13, 16).

In the original script, Sport too was to have been a black character. However, Scorsese and Schrader felt that this would be too provocative and might incite race riots. When Keitel carried out research for the part, he nonetheless discovered that the only pimps he could find were black. In the end he based the look of his character on a pimp from the area where he lived, notably with a long pink fingernail (for his cocaine habit), the big hat and the long hair (a wig which, incidentally, he had to argue for because of the very tight budget).

When Travis arrives back at the cab garage, we see him look at the twenty dollar note and the camera tilts back down as he picks it up. It takes on enormous symbolic significance for Travis, representing Iris's 'imprisonment' and being taken from his pocket twice more in the film (chapters 11 and 21).

8. a date with betsy

ACTION

Travis meets Betsy and takes her to a cinema. He gives her a copy of the Kris Kristofferson album, which she already owns. To her embarrassment, he chooses a porn film for their date and she quickly leaves.

COMMENTARY

In direct contrast to his first encounter with Iris, Travis is again dressed in his red velvet jacket (chapter 5), appearing out of the crowd in slow motion, reminiscent of the first introduction of Betsy to the film (chapter 3). She too is dressed as in that first appearance, all in white. Travis's awkwardness is emphasised by his attempts to give Betsy the present:

```
My record player doesn't work ... I was thinkin'
maybe we could listen to it on your record player.
```

As they walk along the street, they pass the street drummer, Gene Palma, who is there to give the street scene authenticity. It is a quirky touch, unmotivated by the narrative, as he twice appears in big close-up and the sound of his drumming overlaps the visuals loudly as they arrive at the cinema itself. Spotted by Peter Boyle (Wizard), who suggested Scorsese used him in the film, the drummer appears in a shot reminiscent of some documentary-style moments from *Mean Streets* (1973), giving a sense that even when the actors aren't there for *Taxi Driver*, he still will be.

At the cinema, Betsy is appalled at the idea of going to see this film, to which Travis responds that he doesn't know a lot about movies, clearly an understatement. He tries to grab her but she pulls away from him several times, in an echo of Iris trying to shake off Sport (chapter 7).

The cut to Travis's phone call is indicative that several days have passed and features one of the most unconventional shots of the film. As Travis talks, offering to take Betsy to dinner and asking whether she got the flowers he sent he becomes more painful than ever for the audience to watch. At this point, the camera tracks away from him and looks down a corridor into the street. Apparently this was the first shot Scorsese thought of for the film

sickness/health metaphor

and is very unconventional in the sense of being an apparently unmotivated track. At the end of his phone call, however, Travis does walk into the space which the camera is viewing. Again this is a specific deviation from the original screenplay, where she hangs up on him.

In his interview with Mark Cousins, Scorsese described the shot as:

> an emotionally motivated move. It is too painful to watch him go through that humiliation on the phone.
>
> *Scorsese, interviewed for BBC 2, 4/4/1998*

Travis's voice-over restarts, (it is 10 June) moving the viewer on in time, and continues over the tracking shot of the unwanted flowers, to which his phone call has just referred:

`The smell of the flowers only made me sicker. The headaches got worse. I think I've got stomach cancer ... You are only as healthy as you feel.`

The sickness/health metaphor continues through the film, just as he finishes asking Betsy whether she has recovered from the flu (which the audience assumes has just been an excuse not to speak to him), he starts his hypochondria again. Later he will write to his parents about what good health he is in (chapter 18). The real health problem, however, is clearly mental.

9. confrontation

ACTION

Following Betsy's rejection of Travis, he comes to the campaign office to speak to her. Tom tries to shepherd him out as he causes a scene, threatening Tom with violence and telling Betsy she is going to hell.

COMMENTARY

This is a brief scene, which starts very abruptly as Travis bursts through the door. Travis's purposeful march into the campaign office, is accompanied by a tracking shot until Tom tries to prevent him moving further towards Betsy. He has clearly given up trying to 'save' Betsy:

sexual rage

you're in a hell and you're going to die in a hell
like the rest of them.

Travis strikes a martial arts pose as, dressed in his combat jacket, he threatens Tom. The framing is striking here, as he and Tom are central in the background, surrounded by posters for Palantine with Betsy looking on in the foreground. As he leaves, he is chased by the cop that Tom has shouted to, but his voice-over is resigned:

I realise now how much she is just like the others,
cold and distant ... women are like a union.

A union like all others, from which Travis feels excluded. Always the lonely outsider – from the other taxi drivers, in his flat, separated from his passengers, who act sometimes as if he isn't even there, and above all separated from women.

10. curbside cuckold

ACTION

Travis picks up a fare who tells him to drive to a building and then demands that he look up at the silhouette of a woman in a second floor window. He tells Travis that this is his wife, who is having an affair with a black man, that he wants to shoot her and laughs at what his gun could do to her, using particularly violent and repellent images in his conversation.

COMMENTARY

Throughout the sequence, Travis stays silent apart from two moments where he finally acknowledges he can see what the passenger is asking him about. The scene is shot with mainly separate framing and fragmented vision through mirrors. There are parallels in what he wants to do in taking revenge on his wife with Travis's anger with Betsy. This is sexual rage; his talk of using a Magnum .44, not only one of the weapons Travis buys later, but also the (phallic) gun used by Clint Eastwood as *Dirty Harry* (1971).

It is notable that Scorsese himself chose to play this character, originally earmarked for someone else; the levels of violence and sickness conveyed

10. curbside cuckold   narrative & form

by Travis throughout the film are here displayed in equal measure by someone else too. As Kolker puts it:

> the gaze of two psychotics, one the function of the other, join, doubling the viewer's distressed perceptions.
>
> *Kolker, 1988, pp. 191–2*

It also echoes the role Scorsese plays at the end of *Mean Streets* (1973), where he is a hitman, seated in the back of a car.

More significantly, as Lawrence Friedman (1997, pp. 79–80) suggests, it can be viewed as a turning point in the film, where the Scorsese character 'directs the gaze' of both De Niro's character and the audience to the woman in the window. He also directs Travis's future thoughts by suggesting the weapon, which will later be the first weapon he buys from Easy Andy (chapter 13). It becomes the phallic substitute for the impotent Travis and the link is further made later (chapter 21) with Iris, herself known as 'Easy' too, thus linking sex (through the prostitute and the unfaithful wife) and death (through the passenger's threats, the gun which Travis buys and also the gun which lies on Sport's crotch as he lies dead – another Magnum, chapter 27).

11. a word with wizard

ACTION

At the all-night diner, the drivers are telling more tall stories. Travis goes outside with Wizard to ask for advice.

COMMENTARY

Again Travis's separation from others is emphasised as the rest of the drivers swap stories before he comes in and he sits slightly apart from them. When Charlie T asks him for the money he owes him, Travis pointedly separates the twenty dollar note from Sport and puts it back in his pocket. Charlie T calls him 'killer' and makes a gun with his finger and a gun-like noise, foreshadowing the final shoot-out sequence (chapter 27). Outside the diner, Travis is lit in a red haze as the camera pans around him, taking

'bad ideas in my head'

the point-of-view of the black man with chains passing by, at whom Travis stares.

His conversation with Wizard borders on the abstract:

```
I wanna go out and really do something ... I've got
some bad ideas in my head.
```

Wizard intimates that he really doesn't know what Travis is talking about, but nonetheless offers advice:

```
go out, get laid, get drunk, do anything ... relax,
killer you're going to be alright.
```

Again there is irony in this. Travis is not likely to do any of the things suggested, but the idly chosen nickname is going to be completely appropriate. Wizard describes how a man and his job become intertwined, the dialogue essentially a description of Travis himself, with increasingly no life outside his taxi driving and nothing but thwarted attempts to get one. He is the taxi driver of the title and that is all he is.

As they shake hands and Wizard gets in his cab and drives off, Travis is shown through the rear window, a prostitute moving towards him and the military style theme beginning on the soundtrack.

12. running into iris

ACTION

Travis's second encounter with Iris occurs as he is driving along and almost runs her over.

COMMENTARY

The sequence begins with Travis pouring peach brandy onto his cereal as he watches Palantine on TV, an illustration of his decadent lifestyle; Palantine's words:

```
the people are beginning to rule ... [the people]
will rise to an unprecedented swell.
```

change

echo the build-up and explosion which will come from Travis later. Travis drives past the campaign headquarters and Betsy's empty desk is shown from his point of view. As the view cuts to night with Travis dropping off a fare, there is a shock moment when he almost runs over Iris and her friend. His long stare is then followed by him driving slowly and observing them. Once they pick up two men, and the lights change, Travis speeds off.

His voice-over as he drives, again shot in slow motion, passing couples on the pavement describes his feelings:

`loneliness has followed me my whole life ... I'm God's lonely man.`

This quotation from Thomas Wolfe suggests a level of literacy from Travis of which we have hitherto been unaware (he seems to find simpler things impossible to comprehend). It is also significant that he describes himself as having a holy calling. Like other disturbed individuals, he rationalises his actions as a religious duty. One of the most common reasons cited by both real-life and also fictional serial killers for their 'work' is 'God told me to', from Peter Sutcliffe, the 'Yorkshire Ripper', to John Doe in *Seven* (1995). Travis's loneliness is thus converted from futile attempts at connecting with others into a holy calling. As the voice-over continues, the camera tracks around his apartment, past the 'Vote Palantine' posters and the 'I gotta get organezizied' sign, he says:

`My life has taken another turn ... suddenly there is a change.`

This might be said to mark the turning point in the narrative; the audience is given no particular insight into what he intends to do or what exactly motivates him to do it, but Travis seems to decide at this point to turn things around.

13. easy andy

ACTION

Travis goes to a hotel room with an illegal gun salesman, Andy, introduced to him by Dough-Boy. Andy offers him a range of weapons, of which

practising with weapons

Travis buys most. Travis is then shown exercising at home, going through a series of preparations with his weapons and practising at a shooting range.

COMMENTARY

As Christopher Sharrett has noted, each of the guns on offer seems to represent a potentially different type of movie hero:

> The gun-buying scene has many intertextual aspects, presenting a kind of condensed repository of the popular culture that has been a contributing force in Travis's delusions. Travis buys a Walther PPK (James Bond), a snub-nose Smith and Wesson .38 (Mike Hammer), a pocket-sized .25 automatic (also Bond ordnance) and the .44 Magnum (the most popular handgun in America) following the success of *Dirty Harry* (1971).
>
> *Sharrett, 1993, p. 230*

Andy describes what they can do, echoing the Scorsese character earlier (chapter 11). He talks of some of the guns and the holster as if they were females:

isn't that a little honey? ... that's a beauty.

and makes racist comments:

I could sell these to some jungle bunny up in Harlem for 500 dollars.

The overhead shot is used again in this sequence, once at the hotel showing the guns in the case, at the shooting range as he picks them up and then of Travis himself as he does push-ups. Andy's offer of drugs to Travis is fiercely resisted, as was Betsy's suggestion earlier (chapter 5) that he reminded her of the 'pusher' line from the song. Travis sees junkies and dealers as evil and rejects illegal drugs, yet he is constantly pill-popping himself.

Travis tries out guns by pointing them unloaded at people out of the window. Back at his apartment the voice-over begins again; time has

'True Force'

military-style operation

passed (it is 29 June), the flowers are still there, decaying; various rubbish is strewn around the room. Travis is shown doing push-ups, pull-ups and lifting weights; the room has become a gym and the music a semi-fanfare on trumpet, announcing the imminent arrival of Travis's military-style operation:

```
I gotta get in shape now, too much sitting has
ruined my body; too much abuse has gone on for too
long.
```

All this is suggestive of a change of direction, a new purpose and an increase in the tempo of the narrative. Travis has moved from inactive to active and this sequence epitomises this change.

Travis looks at the camera/viewer via staring at a mirror (which is where the audience is positioned). He tenses his arm and puts it over a flame, recalling Charlie in *Mean Streets* (1973) testing his faith in the same way.

Scorsese has talked about Herrmann's construction of the music for this scene:

> 'I hear brass' he [Herrmann] said in a call from London ... he wanted to create the impression of strength, so the [sequences] were scored with brass and percussion. They gave the impression of solidity, the unstoppable aspect of Travis's character. Herrmann understood the film perfectly – the sense of Travis being haunted and obsessed, the inevitable feeling that his obsessions will lead to slaughter, and the realisation that the massacre at the end was not the end of Travis's violence.
>
> *Scorsese, sleeve notes for soundtrack CD*

There is a cut to the shooting range, with the audience positioned as the target, followed by a fast track low shot into Travis's arm outstretched. The quick cuts over the shoulder and the close-up of his face pointing the gun at us emphasise his concentration. Again the final

at the Palantine rally

shoot-out is foreshadowed by his preparation and by the use of the camera itself.

Travis is then shown once again in a porno theatre, pointing his finger in a gun gesture at the screen. On the soundtrack, as he frames his eye with his fingers (rather as Sport will do in a later scene, chapter 20), Travis makes his intentions more explicit:

```
the idea's been growing in my brain for some time.
True force. All the king's men cannot put it
together again.
```

The voice-over overlaps to Travis back in his apartment, now like a cowboy hero, drawing from his holsters, bare chested. The mattress is rolled up, like that of a soldier and he is acting out a series of draws. We see him making weapons, adapting his equipment, creating a dum dum bullet in huge close-up. His preparation is meticulous, reminiscent of both the military and of that for a final shoot-out in a western, such as *A Fistful of Dollars* (1964), itself harking back to Samurai preparations. Most of all he is like the bare chested hero of martial arts films, like Bruce Lee in *Enter the Dragon* (1973).

14. henry krinkle

ACTION

Travis goes to a Palantine rally and stands next to a secret serviceman. He asks about joining the secret service and gives a false name and address. As Palantine arrives, the agent suggests a cameraman takes a shot of Travis, but he escapes in the mêlée.

COMMENTARY

The long held shot of Travis waiting next to the secret serviceman and eventually conversing with him again offers him as excruciatingly embarrassing. His naivete is emphasised as he has made himself so obvious that he cannot be about to do anything terrible. The agent wears dark glasses, which Travis copies as he awaits the next rallies (chapters 18 and 24). The dark glasses function for the characters in different ways: they disguise, they hide the eyes – the giveaway of emotion – but they are also like a child's toy (for Travis it is almost a case of playing at secret agents when he wears them).

His awkward handshake, which echoes meetings with Wizard, Betsy, the cab firm interviewer and later Iris, is this time with the wrong hand, presumably because the other arm contains a weapon. He is wearing a different jacket, green, suggesting readiness for military action. The scene ends with a crane shot as Palantine arrives and Travis leaves.

This scene again deviates from the screenplay in which Tom sees Travis from the podium and points him out to Betsy. This is a significant difference, as in the film, Betsy has no contact with Travis from the point of the confrontation sequence till the very end of the film when she is in his cab. He (and we) see her at the various rallies, but if she had seen him, then the final sequence, where she acknowledges his 'heroism' (chapter 28) would have been impossible, since she would know of his assassination intentions.

15. 'you talkin' to me?'

ACTION

Travis rehearses with his guns in his apartment again.

COMMENTARY

One of the most memorable scenes in cinema, this was largely improvised by De Niro; in the original screenplay it is combined with the sequence of preparation described above and the idea that he is about to try to assassinate the candidate was spelt out more by reference to the mise-en-scène:

```
Tracking shot to wall of Travis's apartment. Camera
moves slowly across wall covered with clippings,
notes, maps, pictures. We now see their contents
clearly:

The wall is covered with Charles Palantine political
```

15. 'you talkin' to me?' narrative & form

paraphernalia; there are pictures of him, newspaper
articles, leaflets, bumper stickers. As the camera
moves along it discovers a sketch of Plaza Hotel,
Kennedy Airport and cut-up sections of city maps
with notations written in. There is a lengthy *New
York Times* clipping detailing the increased Secret
Security Protection during the primaries. A section
pertaining to PALANTINE is underlined. Further along
there is a sheet reading 'travelling schedule' and a
calendar for June with finely written notations
written over the dates.

(screenplay, p. 47)

Little of this is clearly visible in the film itself, though much of it is there in
the background. Here the actual sequence begins with a **zip pan**from the
mirror to Travis talking to himself. The dislocation between Travis's fantasy
image of himself (avenger, courageous, strong, manly, even a federal agent
in disguise) as seen in the mirror, and Travis as seen by the audience as
vulnerable and even childlike, playing guns and dressing up, is emphasised.
Like a child, framed at the side of the image, he seems to be addressing the
audience. He then appears to rotate as if on a turntable and there are **jump
cuts**repeating the shot, just as the voice-over is repeated, partly over the
rotating shot and partly over an overhead shot of him on the bed. Visually
the whole scene is reminiscent of the French New Wave, particularly of
Godard, in its unconventional use of camera, repetition and particularly
jump cuts to disorient the viewer.

The clutter of his apartment reflects the confusion of his mind, though
he identifies with the regulated lifestyle of law and order represented by
the Secret Service. The use of the mirror emphasises the split between
Travis as victim and as victor over an imagined opponent; in his outfit
he addresses both the audience and himself, pointing the gun and
prefiguring the ending, yet his grin and at one point his thin naked
torso make him seem even more childlike as if the whole episode is play.
Despite his arsenal of weapons, the slow speed with which he uses some

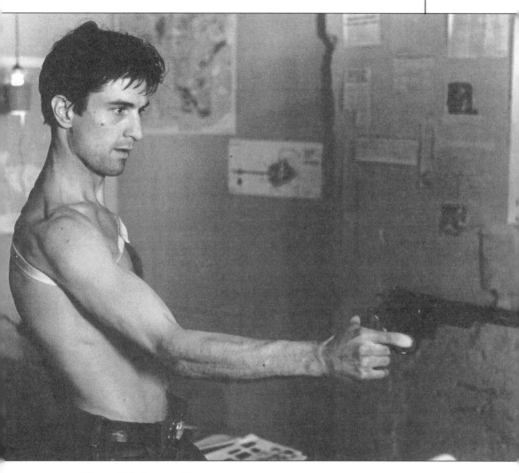

'You talkin' to me?'

of them leaves him vulnerable to being killed himself, and when he curls up on the bed in a foetal posture, shot from above, he once again looks exposed.

'I'm the only one here' he says at one point, which refers not only to his solitude in front of the mirror but also to his state of mind on the margins of society. The motif of the mirror, most central in this sequence, occurs elsewhere in the film, in the cab (throughout), but also in characters who are effectively his 'mirror image', such as Sport (chapter 20) and the man in the cab played by Scorsese (chapter 10).

16. market robbery

ACTION

Travis goes to a late night store and while he is selecting milk, a robber comes in and points a gun at the shopkeeper. Travis calls to him and shoots him dead as he turns around. Travis stands upon him as he checks that he is dead, telling the shopkeeper he does not have a licence for the gun. The shopkeeper tells Travis to go and then beats the dead man's body with a broom handle.

COMMENTARY

Travis drives through the wet streets and through pink-coloured smoke, just like the opening sequence. A police car races by, its siren blaring, as if aware of what is about to happen. This is echoed later when Travis first goes into the building with Iris, when again a siren can be heard (chapter 21).

He knows the shopkeeper and they acknowledge one another by name. A tracking shot behind the counter stops at a view of Travis behind the raider, gun raised. After the shooting, the overhead shot dominates the sequence as we see the raider's body on the floor. Travis has thus inadvertantly begun to wreak his vengeance on the streets, meting out instant punishment.

This is a significant deviation from the screenplay, where the shopkeeper is reluctant to take the blame for Travis's actions and phones the police.

In the film itself, beating the body in a display of hatred is part of the pattern of latent racism in the film (linking with chapters 4, 10, 11 and 13).

17. 'late for the sky'

ACTION

Travis sits at home watching TV. Black people are dancing to Jackson Browne's 'Late for the Sky'. Travis is pointing his Magnum at the dancers, then in a reverse shot of the extreme close-up of the screen, we see him pointing at his own head.

COMMENTARY

The lyrics echo his mental state:

```
close to the end of the feeling we've known
how long have I been sleeping
how long have I been drifting on through the
night ...?
```

After an initial close-up of Travis toying with the gun and looking at the TV set, taken from the position of the set, there is a cut to the reverse angle, an extreme close-up of the programme itself. The TV stands on a crate, again giving a sense of his makeshift existence.

As in other scenes, the sequence begins with a kind of static tableau shot. This is followed, however, by a series of slow tracking shots in; first over Travis's shoulder on the TV set. This continues into what is effectively a track within a track, as the camera within the TV programme itself tracks apparently pointlessly onto a pair of shoes lying on the dance floor. This diversion of attention onto random detail is symptomatic of Travis's condition, endlessly and obsessively picking up on details yet unable to see the whole picture.

There also seems to be a mismatch between the dancing on TV and the music playing. It is as if Travis is listening to the music from another source while the television is on without volume. This is emphasised by the camera

move on

movement around Travis and the way in which the lyrics themselves comment on Travis's state of mind.

The third track of the sequence is into Travis's face. Combined, the three tracking shots give both the sense of restlessness (the camera is never static), but also the sense of delving ever-deeper into the mind of the character.

18. 'dear father and mother'

ACTION

Travis is seated in his cab at the scene of another Palantine rally. We hear part of Palantine's speech and see the campaigners on the stage. In voice-over Travis is writing a card to his parents. The scene ends with a police officer telling him to move on, Travis driving away and an overlap shot to him reading the card he has just completed, once again seated in his apartment.

COMMENTARY

The opening four images here, low off-angle static shots of tall New York buildings, are reminiscent of the opening shots of the sequence where Travis first encounters Betsy (chapter 3), acting as establishing shots but also looking to the sky (itself a link back to the song just heard, which is still fading as the sequence begins). The fourth shot gives diegetic motivation for the speech we hear: a loudspeaker broadcasting Palantine's words. Here he is quoting Walt Whitman:

```
that great American poet, who spoke for us all when
he said 'I am the man, I suffered, I was there'
Today I say to you, we are the people, we suffered,
we were there.
```

Though he goes on to make allusions to the Vietnam war, unemployment, inflation, crime and corruption, the quotation most clearly refers to Travis's state of mind. As the crowd applauds, there is a tilt down to a shot of Travis, wearing dark glasses, in his cab outside a pizza place in a neighbouring street. Palantine can be seen framed in a window allowing

'Dear Father & Mother'

distortion of facts

Travis only a limited view (he can't see his head), typical of how he interprets reality. Betsy is visible in the corner of one of the framed shots.

As the speech continues, Herrmann's brooding theme music begins and Travis's voice-over, writing the card to his parents presents the viewer with another version of his point of view.

His distortion of the facts (about his state of health, relationship with Betsy and work for the government) is obviously apparent to the audience while the card prefigures the 'thank you' letter he will receive from Iris's parents at the end of the film (chapter 28). The absence of family in the film is only emphasised more by such moments. In some ways it is a surprise to learn that he indeed has parents, but no surprise that one card has to act as a catch-all for several annual occasions.

The camera crosses the crowd and the platform in two separate pans, neither of which clearly reveal Palantine's face. As Travis speaks his line about Betsy, we see her arm in the corner of the frame.

The voice-over continues after he is moved on by the police officer as the camera takes the viewer back to Travis's apartment. This overlapping sound masks a variety of shifts in time and space in the film, but also serves to emphasise the monotony of his existence, echoed in turn by the drumbeat. The image of the bars behind him reinforces the sense of his entrapment; the ineptitude of his message is emphasised by his line:

`I hope no-one has died.`

19. tv critic

ACTION

Travis is in his apartment once again, watching a daytime soap and pointing his Magnum at the screen. He pushes the TV with his boot, but it tilts too far and crashes over, exploding instantly.

COMMENTARY

Unlike the previous TV-watching scene, most of this scene is shot side-on, though still with the camera constantly restless. As Travis pushes at the set with his boot, there is a visual echo of the sign on the wall which he mentioned earlier to Betsy – 'one of these days I'm going to get organezizied' which features a cartoon image of someone with their feet up. The Palantine slogans are also clearly visible in the shot.

The characters on the soap talk about their marriage being illegal, 'but in the eyes of God we are married' perhaps referring to Travis's view of justice coming from a higher authority than the law.

As Travis reacts to the pointless act of destroying the TV, his head in his hands, the music begins again and there is a dissolve to an extreme close-up of Travis's reaction. As in other uses of the dissolve in the film, this is an unusual edit in that conventionally it signals the passing of time, yet here none has passed.

20. looking for action

ACTION

Travis returns to the street where he previously saw Iris. He speaks to her and she sends him over to the pimp to negotiate. He agrees the price with Sport, who is suspicious that he may be an undercover policeman.

COMMENTARY

The camera pans across behind Travis, sitting in the cab, seen only in silhouette swigging from a bottle in a bag, revealing Iris and her friend coming into shot from around the next corner. This clearly simulates Travis's point of view as they pass across in front of the cab, with the camera panning back at the same time. As Travis gets out of the cab to talk to Iris, there is a cut to a shot of the three of them walking along.

Iris is dressed in her big floppy hat, coloured sunglasses, a thin blouse with plenty of flesh revealed and a pair of red hot pants, while Travis wears a check shirt, jeans, boots and dark glasses. Iris's outfit makes her look like a hippy, while Travis is reminiscent of a cowboy. Sport/Matthew has his tall hat, a vest and chain with long black trousers, giving him the air of an Indian chief.

'Catch you later, copper'

As Iris tells Travis to speak to Matthew/Sport (the pimp) about the possibility of 'action', she walks out of shot. The conversation between Travis and Sport takes place without camera movement and lasts for over one and a half minutes, with the entire shot from leaving the cab lasting over two minutes. This represents one of the longest static shots in the entire film. At first Sport assumes Travis is a policeman, then from his dress and naivete that he is a cowboy. Both are among the roles that Travis enacts; the 'vigilante cop' figure roaming the streets constantly looking and making notes and ultimately meting out justice and as the Wayne-like avenger who comes to take on the Indian-lookalike Sport.

When Sport is convinced that he is a customer, his description of Iris's services make her the ultimate cheap object. This view of women is both diametrically opposite to Travis's objectification of Betsy as angelic, but also aligned with his experience of porn films.

Even by the end of their conversation, Sport is still inclined to the possibility that Travis is an undercover cop, making the gesture with his fingers in a frame around his eye, an echo of the use of the gunsight in the Easy Andy sequence (chapter 13). Sport pretends to shoot imaginary pistols at Travis in a moment that prefigures Travis's finger at his own head at the end of the film (chapter 28). This moment is reminiscent of moments in *Mean Streets* (1973) and *Alice Doesn't Live Here Anymore* (1974), both also featuring Keitel.

In the final shot of sequence, the camera tilts up the tenement building to the sky as the sound of a siren wails by, a shot which will be repeated at the start of the Sport and Iris sequence (chapter 23).

21. $10 room

ACTION

Travis follows Iris into the building and pays a man $10 for the use of the room. Iris asks him what he wants to do and he stops her, telling her this is no job for someone of her age to do. She does not remember their previous encounter. He asks to see her again for breakfast the next day.

desire to 'rescue'

COMMENTARY

Inside the building we start with a tracking shot of Travis and Iris walking down the corridor. They are framed centrally and at the rear of the shot is the man who will charge Travis for the room. This sequence refers forward to Travis's next visit, when he will shoot this man's hand off in the same corridor (chapter 27).

Iris's room has hippy qualities about it, with the beaded curtains, candles, rock star posters and cushions, as well as a predominance of feminine colours in the mise-en-scène. Her own outfit (which Jodie Foster was particularly uncomfortable about wearing) carries echoes of Janis Joplin, a rock singer who died shortly after her Woodstock performance.

Travis pauses behind the door before entering, leading Iris to turn to beckon him in, as if she is in charge. Her two names, like those of Sport/Matthew each carry quite different connotations. Just as Matthew derives from the apostle and Sport from notions of recreation, so Iris, an old fashioned name carrying associations with nature (a flower) contrasts with 'Easy', which clearly indicates her status as sexual plaything.

His rejection of her advances, stopping her from undressing any further and pushing her away as she tries to undo his trousers, becomes more vigorous as the scene progresses, as if there is some attempt to tease the audience into the horrified view that something might happen between them after all.

When Iris says that she does not like her real name, there is a sense of it representing her rejection of her Midwest childhood, from which she has run away. This is echoed in the next sequence as she accuses him of being 'square' for wanting an idealised version of childhood back for her.

Travis's acknowlegement that he has tried and failed to persuade her to escape is followed by his awkwardness in proffering a handshake. The music wells up in the love theme, indicating the parallels between this meeting and that with Betsy earlier. On one level, this is of course ironic, but on another it represents the same twisted desire to do good on the part of Travis. In both cases, he believes he can 'rescue' them.

As he leaves, though, the music becomes more ominous. In the dirty brown corridor, he hands over the symbolic screwed up twenty dollar note which he has kept for so long, saying:

```
this is yours, spend it right.
```

The slow-motion camera foreshadows the camera use next time he will be there and as he walks down the stairs the man calls after him:

```
come back any time cowboy.
```

to which he replies with dramatic significance:

```
I will.
```

22. breakfast with iris

ACTION

The next day, Travis meets Iris and they go to a cafe.

COMMENTARY

For this sequence Iris is dressed differently, wearing jeans and showing less flesh. Her hair is not so flamboyant and she has no hat. There are clear echoes of the sequence eating pie with Betsy, particularly in some of the framing and camerawork, yet it is very different too. There is no anxiety on Travis's part that he made a 'good choice' this time, and Iris tipping jam and sugar on her toast and trying on different pairs of sunglasses emphasises her childlike qualities.

Her claim that her parents hate her is contrasted with the letter received by Travis at the end. But throughout the sequence, Travis for once comes over as a knowledgeable sensible person, advising her to get out. Her naivete is emphasised by her comments on 'Women's lib' and astrology, but there is some sense of her taking notice of Travis too.

She questions his right to define her life:

```
What makes you so high and mighty ... don't you
ever try looking at your own eyeballs in the mirror?
```

Travis and Iris

tender or creepy

An ironic question given his own self-obsession throughout the film (especially chapter 15) and apt too, coming from someone whose name also refers to part of the eye (Iris).

When he asks her what she will do to effect an escape, he makes clear his lack of faith in the police and then his anger rises as he describes his view of Sport. He later sticks to his word in offering to pay for her to escape.

The sequence ends with a shot of Travis once again in his cab, looking up at the tenement building in an echo of the shot which ended the 'looking for action' sequence. It links with the next scene in the sense of perhaps representing Travis imagining Sport and Iris together or possibly suggesting that he knows that they are in the building.

23. dancing with sport

ACTION

Sport puts on a record and dances with Iris. He tells her how important she is to him and how much he depends upon her.

COMMENTARY

This sequence is unique in that it is the only one in the film not to feature Travis. The audience is relentlessly offered Travis's point of view and scenes of his embarrassing behaviour, yet here is allowed to see something he does not.

Whether the sequence is read as one of tenderness or of creepiness has been debated. Travis's assumption that anything would be better for this girl than prostitution is not one that she wholly shares. Iris told Travis in the previous sequence that Sport had never treated her badly, never beating her up (presumably unlike the other pimps and prostitutes she knows).

In a film devoid of human connection, Friedman argues that this is the one moment of tenderness, the only on-screen evocation of 'home' in the film: 'Iris's, like Travis's parental home exists only as an offscreen cliche as does the commune in Vermont that Iris offhandedly suggests' (Friedman, 1997, p. 70).

23. dancing with sport narrative & form

Other viewers have recoiled at the dance between Iris and her pimp, mouthing sickeningly sentimental platitudes. Either way, what is shown to the audience for the first time since the scene between Tom and Betsy, is a world not seen through Travis's eyes. Perhaps both 'couples' represent a threat to Travis's masculinity; in both cases, he expresses to the females his distaste for the males.

Travis has clearly sown the seeds of doubt in Iris's mind, as she tells Sport she does not enjoy what she is doing. Here the music Sport puts on the turntable represents a shift from non-diegetic to diegetic, as Herrmann's love theme begins, though the context of the scene might lead some viewers to describe it as the 'sleazy' theme. Sport continues talking throughout in what Keitel described as 'like a Barry White song', much of the dialogue being improvised by Keitel.

Their dance is interrupted (for the viewer) by the noise of gunfire and there is a very fast sequence of shots of Travis at the shooting gallery. These gunshots almost give a sense of waking abruptly from a bad dream, since they partially overlap the dancing footage, perhaps suggesting the whole sequence is one of Travis's fantasies. Each shot brings Travis closer to the camera; there is a series of shots too of the target and another of the overhead shots of the carefully patterned layout of his weapons as he picks them up in turn. Again this represents his need for order and organisation, for everything to be done in a particular way.

The cut back to his apartment to the completion of his religious-style ritual, heating and applying boot polish, burning the remains of the flowers, getting dressed, with a clean white shirt instead of the check he has worn previously, sticking his knife to his boot all represents a severance of connections: the flowers of emotional ties with Betsy, the ripping of the shirt and the sticky tape like a tearing-up of the links with society.

His note to Iris emphasises his preparedness as does the voice-over:

> Now I see it clearly, my whole life has been
> pointing in one direction. There never has been any
> choice for me.

It also reminds the audience of his childishness, through his stuttering reading and his barely literate handwriting. He is a child in an adult's world, but one acting out sadistic fantasies.

24. the palantine rally

ACTION

Columbus circle, Palantine is speaking at his biggest rally yet. Travis is looking on and is revealed to have shaved his head, mohawk fashion. As Palantine leaves the podium, Travis makes his way through the crowd and starts to pull his gun from his jacket. Spotted by secret servicemen, he aborts his mission and runs off. He drives quickly downtown.

COMMENTARY

One of the rally's most striking visual features is the way in which Palantine raises his arms in an echo of the statue behind him, which serves to make him look ridiculous. He stands out from the crowd in his dress and through his posture: when not likened to the statue, he stands hands on hips in an echo of the gunfighter at the end of a western, in this case waiting for the 'Indian'. Indeed, the cutting in this sequence almost presents it as a face-off or showdown. The rapid cutting sets up a sense of impending danger.

Travis's arrival is a memorable moment; he is shown from the waist down as he steps from the cab and the camera tracks at waist height along a row of onlookers till it pauses on Travis. The camera tilts up as he pops a pill, revealing him wearing his dark glasses and a mohican haircut.

The haircut both shifts him from cowboy to Indian and also acts as a reference to the Vietnam war. Paul Schrader was told of soldiers in the Special Services who would cut their hair into a mohawk before going into battle in the jungle. Here Travis is a cross between them, armed as a 'man with a mission' in his green combat jacket, but also out of place in the city.

Travis grins inanely as he applauds and there is a cut to firstly a shot of Betsy, besuited on the platform and then a long shot of Travis at the back of the crowd, standing out clearly. Palantine's speech is full of the inanities

plan B

he has uttered throughout the campaign. The camera pans across other figures on stage, including the secret serviceman to whom Travis had spoken earlier.

As Palantine leaves the podium to walk through the crowd, the camera follows Travis's passage at first, then intercuts between Palantine and aides coming towards the camera and Travis. As the grinning Travis unzips his jacket to pull out a gun, there is a zip pan to the secret serviceman who spots him. This is a moment of disorientation for the viewer, just as there is chaos in the scene. In the mêlée, Travis makes his escape.

So why does he try to kill Palantine? On one level, Palantine might be seen to represent the father-figure to Betsy, who must be destroyed, either to free her, or purely for revenge. She is identified in Travis's mind with Palantine, being visually associated through the posters at the campaign office and here seated by him at the rally.

On another level, Palantine is the typically deceitful and unreliable politician in a corrupt era, representing Travis's disillusion at the apparent lack of desire to clean up the streets. The candidate's actions can never match his rhetoric; he uses this slogan 'we are the people', identifying himself with the common man, yet as soon as he comes into contact with one, he is uneasy and embarrassed.

The attempt aborted, Travis returns home; bare chested, he makes preparations for plan B, swigging down another tablet with a Budweiser. He seems to transfer his rage now to Sport, another 'father-figure'. He had put aside the money to set Iris free and announced his own death in the note, but now his desire to fulfil his 'heroic' destiny takes a new turn.

25. 'suck on this'

ACTION

As Travis races through the streets at nightfall in the cab, a mafioso arrives to collect money from Sport, prior to visiting Iris. Travis arrives at Sport's doorway for their second conversation. Sport doesn't remember him now that he looks different. Travis shoots him with the words 'suck on this'. Travis sits down in a nearby doorway on some steps.

COMMENTARY

From leaving the cab to sitting down, it is all one take, similar to the previous conversation between the pair, leaving the viewer distant from the action. The only camera movement follows Travis in and out from the doorway. On the wall behind Sport is a poster for the other candidate, Goodwin, indicating the all-pervasive nature of the election as much as that of the 'filth' of the city.

Now Travis is no longer the cowboy but has himself completed the transition to Indian, with the Mohawk against the long hair and headband of the Apache. In Westerns, the battle between rival tribes had taken the form of good and bad Indians in the past, but here it becomes almost grotesque. The sequence is also evocative of *The Searchers* (1956, see Contexts: Genre and Influences), where John Wayne as Ethan Edwards adopts the Indian's tactics in scalping his victim, as part of his quest to restore his niece to white society.

Some viewers have found it odd that Travis should sit down after shooting Sport, but this action was motivated by De Niro's research into killers, from which he learned that it is not uncommon for them to stay at the scene rather than hastening away.

26. shooting gallery

ACTION

Travis goes into the building where he went before with Iris. As the old man who took the ten dollars before comes towards him, Travis points the gun and shoots off his hand. As he reloads, Sport shoots him in the neck. Travis responds with several bullets; the old man tries to get him and then the mafioso comes out and shoots Travis in the arm. Travis responds with a series of shots to the head; the mafioso falls back in the room and brings down the beaded curtain. Iris is screaming. The old man chases Travis into the room and as they wrestle on the floor, Travis draws his knife and stabs him in the hand before drawing another gun and shooting him dead. Iris sobs as he tries to unload the guns into his own head, but he is out of bullets.

bloodletting and sacrifice

COMMENTARY

This sequence is particularly spectacular and was very complex to construct in such a confined area (see Contexts: Production). Filmed at a variety of different speeds which help give the eerie effect, the sequence featured so much splattering blood that Scorsese had to desaturate the colours on the request of both the MPAA (Motion Pictures Association of America) and Columbia Pictures in order to get an 'R' rather than an 'X' rating. Scorsese himself felt that this made the sequence more effective rather than less, though Michael Chapman, the cinematographer, disagreed: 'I find it very sad because the original stuff looks like a Rauschenberg and the colours are incredibly vivid' (*Making Taxi Driver*, 1988).

The soundtrack echoes with the voice of the old man threatening to kill Travis; this, coupled with the emphasis on the sound of blood spurting out and the use of slow motion puts across a dreamlike state and again gives us the sense of Travis's point of view. The sequence was in some ways inspired by films like *The Wild Bunch* (1969) with its suicidal glory and Peckinpah-like shoot-out effects. The notion of bloodletting and sacrifice is a key element in Scorsese's films (see Style).

27. 'bang, bang, bang'

ACTION

Amidst all the carnage Travis lies slumped on the sofa. As the police enter, guns drawn, Travis lifts his finger to his temple in a pistol like gesture and mouths the noise of it firing. The camera leaves the scene with a high tracking shot in slow motion and a series of dissolves takes the viewer out into the street where a crowd has gathered.

COMMENTARY

For Travis it has all been a suicide mission, evident both in the words of the note he left Iris and by his attempt to discharge the empty gun into his own head. In forming his bloody hand into a pistol and mimicking shots, it is clear that Travis's mission extends even to exorcizing the demons within himself. His gesture echoes many others in the film (chapters 13, 15, 19 and 20) yet it is an empty gesture (Travis has no more bullets, so the finger stands in for the gun), yet it would complete a ritual appropriate to the noble hero of Eastern culture.

This sequence has been much debated; indeed, the director and the writer differ in their own intentions with it. In the screenplay, (p. 86) there is a 'note' that explains Schrader's intentions:

The screenplay has been moving at a reasonably realistic level until this prolonged slaughter. The slaughter itself is a gory extension of violence, more surreal than real.

The slaughter is the moment Travis has been heading for all his life, and where this screenplay has been heading for over 85 pages. It is the release of all that cumulative pressure; it is a reality unto itself. It is the psychopath's Second Coming.

In later films, Schrader makes the ritual self-sacrifice a centrepiece (notably *Mishima*, 1985), but here it is almost parodied as Travis has to mime it grinning. Martin Scorsese indicates a different intention:

> I wanted the violence at the end to be as if Travis had to keep killing all these people in order to stop them once and for all. Paul saw it as a kind of Samurai 'death with honor' - that's why De Niro attempts suicide - and he felt that if he'd directed the scene, there would have been tons of blood all over the walls, a more surrealistic effect. What I wanted was a Daily News situation, the sort you read about every day: 'Three men killed by lone man who saves young girl from them.'
>
> *Scorsese, 1989, p. 63*

Thus in a sense there is a conflict between a realistic tabloid version of events and an expressionistic quasi-religious one.

Yet as well as being readable in terms of a parody of the 'death with honour' motif and the inevitable catharsis for Travis's anger at the city, the catharsis

scene can be viewed as a substitute sexual consummation. The impotent hero, rejected by the woman of his dreams, his pent-up sexual frustrations leading him to porn cinemas and playing with phallic weaponry, finally arrives at the brothel. Yet here his moral code prevents him from undertaking a sexual encounter with the underage prostitute he has paid for; instead he shoots his weapons to free her and obtains the release he has craved throughout, jealously destroying the men who surround and exploit her.

A break with Travis's point of view takes place in the cut from the big close-up of his finger pointing to his temple and his grinning face to the entry of the police via the overhead shot. This shot both completes the pattern of overhead shots in the film with a spectacular slow tracking shot and gives a more detached overview of the scene, either a 'God's eye view' or perhaps the floating soul of the dead. Six dissolves take us to the outside, including shots of blood-spattered walls and stairs, as well as a close-up of Sport's body with the gun in a phallic gesture. This graphically illustrates the consequences of Travis's actions.

The tension that has been building for Travis has been building for the audience too; the catharsis of the shoot-out for him is also catharsis for the audience, yet in taking the audience through the dissolves to reveal the consequences of his actions, the camera is distancing the viewer from Travis. The dramatic crane shot over the street to finish the sequence reveals paramedics arriving and prostitutes trying to get into the building, almost like news footage of the event.

28. 'dear mr bickle'

ACTION

Travis is recovering in bed. As the camera pans around his room to reveal a series of newspaper cuttings and finally a handwritten letter, we hear a voice reading its contents, thanking Travis for saving Iris.

In the final sequence, Travis is outside the St Regis Hotel with the other cabbies. A fare arrives and as Travis gets into the driver's seat, she is revealed as Betsy. She acknowledges seeing him in the papers and when

black comedy?

she gets out he refuses to take payment. As he drives away, he suddenly darts a look into the rear view mirror as if he has spotted something.

COMMENTARY

The first newspaper cutting shows an overhead plan of the room where Travis wreaked havoc, almost like a set plan for the filmmakers. The newspapers are the popular tabloids, two carrying the same picture of Bickle (the image which appears on his cab badge) and one with a picture of Iris's parents (played by Scorsese's parents). Their expression of gratitude is echoed in the deadpan voice-over which reports on Iris's progress and thanks him for his heroism.

This notion of the construction of celebrity is one which Scorsese returns to, particularly in his use of De Niro's characters; in *Raging Bull* (1980) and *New York, New York* (1977) it is celebrity status which leads to the destruction of the central character's relationships with others and ultimately their destruction of themselves. In *The King of Comedy* (1982) the desire for celebrity status is finally realised through illegal means (a kidnapping) and the 'hero' ends up jailed yet famous as a result of media coverage.

Friedman sees the press coverage representing a society:

> that is arguably as psychotic as its new-found hero: Travis's media-made celebrity would be funny if it were not so scary. There is an element of black comedy after all in the tabloids and in the banality of the letter that confer heroism on Travis ... What is truly horrifying, however, is that the media grant public sanction to Travis's private fantasies. It is akin to glorifying Norman Bates, the similarly psychotic killer in that quintessential modern horror movie, *Psycho*. There is no stronger cinematic correlation between sex and violence than *Psycho*'s famous showerscene. But unlike *Taxi Driver*, *Psycho* ends with its crazed killer locked in a cell not loosed on the streets.
>
> Friedman, 1997, p. 86

The newspaper cuttings themselves seem to work sequentially, from the apartment plan to Travis being critical in hospital, to Iris's parents, to Travis

'the film is a loop'

recovering, to his release from hospital and finally to the letter from the Steensmas.

The drivers are all still involved in their casually sexist conversations, Travis is driving again, his grin and his haircut intact, but now Betsy apparently admires his actions, 'I read about you in the papers, how are you?' Her eyes fixed on him throughout, seen in the mirror. His reply is distinctly ironic for the audience given what has been witnessed:

Oh it was nothing really, papers always blow these things up.

He drops her in a leafy suburb and now it is her turn to feel awkward, not knowing what to say. But he simply grins and lets her off the fare. The love theme has played throughout, but in the final shots, there is a return to the ominous music.

In the sleeve notes to the soundtrack album, Scorsese describes his request to Herrmann for a musical moment of emphasis for this sequence:

> In one of the last exchanges we ever had, I told him I needed a little sting for the shot at the end of the picture when Travis suddenly looks back in the mirror – the sure sign that he was still a ticking time bomb. He recorded it on the glockenspiel, and when I listened to the playback I thought it wasn't quite right. 'Run it backwards' he said. As usual he was right.
>
> *Martin Scorsese, sleevenotes to soundtrack album*

The moment undercuts any notion that the killings have functioned cathartically for Travis and question the whole nature of celebrity conferred upon him by the press. It is clear that we are back where we started:

> The film is a loop ... it begins where it ends, nothing has changed, his pathology is still in place.
>
> *Paul Schrader, in Scene by Scene for BBC2*

style

Much of *Taxi Driver* arose from my feeling that movies are really a kind of dream-state or like taking dope. And the shock of walking out of the theater into broad daylight can be terrifying. I watch movies all the time and I am also very bad at waking up. The film was like that for me – that sense of being almost awake.

Martin Scorsese, 1989, p. 54

mise-en-scène

In any film, it is often the mise-en-scène which we remember most above other elements of the film's form and style. The sets and locations, the costumes, the lighting, the colours and particular objects may well stick in our minds long after other elements of the film have been forgotten.

The mise-en-scène of *Taxi Driver* is particularly important in the establishment of mood and atmosphere. The New York locations, with rainy streets at night and steam pouring from drains, give a real sense of the nightmare world which Travis inhabits. The rain too reminds the audience of the metaphoric cleansing of the city which Travis threatens from the start ('someday a real rain will come').

Travis's apartment is a grimy down-at-heel environment, looking temporary, appropriate for the character who lives there and expressive of his lifestyle. Similarly, Iris's room, with its mixture of posters of rock icons, representative of an 'alternative' lifestyle (the 'commune in Vermont') and candles, giving a semi-religious look, indicates the contradictions in her character. Linked with the use of locations is the lighting style of much of the film, with pools of light in an otherwise dark world giving an impression of a descent into hell, a feature borrowed from film noir (see Contexts: Genre and Influences) and German expressionism.

motifs

Objects, costumes and other visual features which carry significance in a film are known as motifs. There are a number of such features which recur during *Taxi Driver* and which carry a great deal of resonance. There is the cab itself, the 'iron coffin' as Schrader describes it, which becomes an extension of Travis, looming monstrously out of the smoke and acting like a metaphor for the pointlessness of existence as Travis drives round and round the city, taking others to their destination but always just taking him back to where he started, ready to start all over again.

Even when Travis is not out driving, taxis are constantly appearing in the frame, as in the cafe scene with Betsy, reminding the viewer of their endless motion. It becomes Travis's means of existence (it pays his wages), but also at times his only reason to live (he becomes the job, as Wizard suggests). It is also the means by which he encounters the other major characters in the film and his way of seeing the world, observing everyone from his driver's seat.

The mirrors (in the car and in the apartment) serve to fragment characters (Travis sees parts of people in his rear view mirror and talks to himself in the mirror at home). The meter in the cab acts like a timepiece in the film, constantly clicking away as time passes, symbolising the life that is passing Travis by. It has the literal function of telling the passengers how much the fare will be, but its function for the audience is different (telling us about Travis).

The guns and the finger positioned as if a gun appear periodically as the film moves towards its climax; from the salesman sequence to the shooting range to the finger pointed at the cinema screen to the gun pointed at the TV set, the motif of the gun is preparing us for the final bloodbath and the mockery of the close-up of Travis with his finger to his temple. His rehearsals in his apartment, his two encounters with Sport, the shooting in the shop all build towards the inevitable moment when Travis explodes into action. It is the sequence with the passenger played by Scorsese which perhaps first sows the seeds of this, as he describes what his gun could do and expresses the rage which Travis feels.

The banknote, which is given to Travis by Sport, for a job that Travis doesn't have to do (driving Iris) becomes symbolic of Iris and her 'imprisonment' as he sees it. Travis decides to hang on to it, finally ritually handing it over after his first full meeting with her, again in payment for a job not done (he doesn't want sex with her).

The costumes in a film will be used to carry significance; here in particular, Travis's combat jacket tells the audience about his past and points towards the ending; Betsy's white dress echoes the voice-over description of her ('like an angel') but the rest of her costumes tend to point towards a smart world with which Travis can have no real contact. Iris's outfit both displays her as the prostitute and carries echoes of the hippie world. The sunglasses, which act as a disguise for both Travis and the secret servicemen, become a signifier of childishness for both Travis and Iris.

Travis's mohawk too becomes part of the film's formal system both in the way it signifies his move into action and as part of a series of references to cowboys and indians (Sport's remarks to Travis and his own Apache appearance). It also functions to physically mark out his difference from the other people at the rally, symbolising his madness against their 'normality'.

character

The main characters in the film all have a clear purpose in developing the narrative. Travis is the protagonist whose actions drive the narrative forward, but it is the two women who become his focus at different points in the film. His desire for Betsy distracts him momentarily from his obsession with the city ('out of this filthy mess'), but his goal is still to rescue her from it. When she rejects him, he shifts his goal to punishing her symbolic father-figure, Palantine, as revenge. His second quest becomes the wish to rescue Iris, which involves punishment of her older lover/pimp and by extension father-figure, Sport, who along with his cronies represents most explicitly the 'filth' of the city.

Yet Travis cannot be considered a simple hero-figure. The audience is given such complex access to his point of view that a simple response of supporting his vigilante actions is unlikely. In particular, the ending of the film, in which he is hailed as a hero, is set against the evidence to which the viewer has had access. The final 'sting' in the music, when he does a double take in the mirror as the final credits are about to roll, undercuts any notion that the story is all over.

camera and editing

The distinctive qualities of *Taxi Driver* as a film has much to do with the conventionally 'invisible' features, the camerawork and the editing. The camera is very restless, just like Travis; in almost any scene in the film, there is evidence to be found of this, through tilts, pans and tracks. As discussed elsewhere (see Narrative and Form), there are some highly distinctive uses of the camera too, which break with continuity editing to the extent that the viewer is drawn to the point of asking 'what's this shot about?', as in the alka seltzer shot and the phone call camera movement. These shots are unmotivated by the action but do tend to have a more expressionist function, taking us into the mind of the character and reflecting how he sees the world.

The pattern of overhead shots throughout the film has been discussed at length in Narrative and Form and these can be seen to function formally in a similar way to poetry, acting like rhymes across the film. The most striking use of camera in *Taxi Driver* is probably the way in which its speed is varied, producing the strange atmosphere of slow motion, particularly in the opening and in the shoot-out sequence. This other-worldly feeling is indicative of Travis's nightmare state. It also produces a haunting grace and beauty for the viewer, particularly in its representation of New York.

The camera also uses point-of-view techniques very frequently in the film, from driver's eye views of the road and traffic lights to shots where the camera is quite literally mounted on the side of the cab. This all helps the spectator to get caught up in a complex relationship with Travis, sharing his point of view, yet being aware of being dragged into it.

The editing uses similarly unconventional devices to tell the story; the use of the dissolve (see Narrative and Form, Chapters 2, 19 and 27) is particularly striking, as is the jump cut, a technique borrowed from Godard and the French New Wave (see Narrative and Form, Chapter 15). Just as the camera draws attention to itself in *Taxi Driver,* so too does the editing and like the camerawork, the editing reflects the character of Travis.

themes

Loneliness, obsession and violence are three key themes of *Taxi Driver.* In addition, the film explores a number of areas, such as the construction of celebrity, of which the ending here offers something of a critique, masculinity in crisis, sickness and disease (both the rotten city and the sickness Travis sees in himself) and cleansing (through water and violence).

The job of a taxi driver is itself a metaphor for loneliness; the driver, separated by a screen, is treated as a nobody by his passengers who do anything they want on the back seat. Travis drives around the city alone, walks alone, lives alone, visits the ultimate lonely place, the porn cinema and sits motionless in the front of his cab as others talk from the back seat. As he says, he is 'God's lonely man'. This loneliness leads on to obsession, with Travis's obsessive desire to clean up the streets becoming mixed with his obsessions with first Betsy and then Iris.

It is the theme of violence which emerges from these twin themes. The blood-letting of the ending finds echoes in other Scorsese films, with a kind of redemption through violence. In *Mean Streets* (1973) there is a bloody ending with a hitman (played by Scorsese) in the back of a car, shooting the protagonist, Charlie (Harvey Keitel) in the street. In *Raging Bull* (1980) it is there throughout the fight scenes, and more recently in *Bringing Out the Dead* (1999) in the way the central character, Frank (Nicholas Cage), gets himself covered in the blood of the victims with whom he comes into contact as a paramedic. Its significance is most obvious in *The Last Temptation of Christ* (1988) where the crucifixion represents the supreme sacrifice, but in all the films mentioned, there is a religious undertone to the blood-letting. In *Taxi Driver* it is 'God's Lonely man' carrying out his 'ordained' mission.

contexts

production

Paul Schrader's original script for *Taxi Driver* originally attracted the interest of director Brian De Palma, who thought it was great writing but found it hard to see how it could be directed. He passed the script to producer Michael Phillips, who along with his wife Julia and Tony Bill were preparing *The Sting* for Universal. They took out an option on the script for $1000 and Martin Scorsese made it clear that he wanted to direct the project. However, the script was left in limbo for nearly three years, because none of the major studios wanted to risk it, as it was so dark a project, and also because Scorsese himself was not yet a proven director.

The success of *Mean Streets* (1973) led to demand for Scorsese to direct projects and the triumph of *The Sting* (1973, winning seven Oscars and taking $80 million at the box office) gave the Phillips more clout. They agreed to Scorsese directing the film provided De Niro played the lead, a role which had already been considered for both Jeff Bridges and Neil Diamond! Scorsese's next film with the Phillips, *Alice Doesn't Live Here Anymore* (1974), got good reviews and an Oscar for Ellen Burstyn, while De Niro won an Oscar for *The Godfather: Part II* (1974). This all combined to make the package look feasible. Julia Phillips persuaded executives at Columbia that if things didn't work out, Steven Spielberg, now a household name through *Jaws* (1975), would take over the project. The studio agreed to a budget of $1.5 million, later rising to $1.9 million.

De Niro was very keen on the project as he had always wanted to write a similar script and told Schrader that he had even gone himself on occasions to the UN and fantasised about assassinating diplomats (Biskind, 1998, p. 295)! Moreover, despite his star power following his Oscar he was still prepared to work for the originally agreed salary of $35,000, slightly more than Schrader's fee and about half of Scorsese's, and a very low price to pay for a rising star in 1975.

production

To put these figures in some kind of perspective, other budgets of the time include: $7 million for *The Exorcist*, $9.5 million for *Star Wars*, $10 million for *Jaws*, with the average for the period at around $8 million.

Schrader worked on rewriting the script, discussing the project with critic Pauline Kael, who did not think at this stage that De Niro could carry a film quite yet. He made use of a range of sources, including literary (Dostoevsky), filmic (Bresson) and real-life (Arthur Bremer's diary).

While rewriting the script, Schrader was reading press reports of the case of Arthur Bremer, who attempted in 1972 to kill Alabama governor George Wallace. The case at least partly influenced his thinking about the portrayal of the character. Bremer was a lonely figure, living in his car and stalking President Nixon. When he failed to penetrate Nixon's security he turned his attention to Wallace. Bremer kept a diary which was subsequently found and revealed an obsessive desire to gain attention, if not celebrity status through killing a famous politician. Given the series of such killings in the USA in the 1960s, such a desire by a disenchanted loner was not surprising.

While revising the script, one night in a New York hotel, Schrader met a girl in the bar. She turned out to be both a drug addict and an underage prostitute. Schrader immediately realised she could be the model for Iris, so he got her to stay till morning, when he introduced her to Scorsese over breakfast, from where much of the material for the breakfast scene in the film was drawn, even down to the sugar on the bread.

The girl herself appears in the film as Iris's friend.

Scorsese doubted that the film would gain a great deal of success, or indeed to start with, a budget:

> In fact, for a while we even thought of doing it on black and white videotape! Certainly we felt it would be a labour of love rather than any kind of commercial success – shoot very quickly in New York, finish it in Los Angeles, release it and then bounce back into *New York, New York*, on which we'd already begun pre-production.
>
> *Scorsese, 1989, p. 54*

production contexts

Filming took place throughout the summer of 1975, but the low budget and limited time in real locations led to a lot of compromise in the shooting process:

> Because of the low budget, the whole film was drawn out on storyboards, even down to medium close-ups of people talking, so that everything would connect. I had to create this dream-like quality in those drawings. Sometimes the character himself is on a dolly, so that we look over his shoulder as he moves towards another character, and for a split second the audience would wonder what was happening.
>
> *Scorsese, 1989, p. 54*

Much of the filming was done by crouching in the back of the cab, which actually helped the claustrophobic feel; the documentary look was often the result of the second unit under David Nichols shooting on the streets. The two main indoor locations, Travis's apartment and the brothel, were situated in an old condemned building.

No editing was done while shooting. Marcia Lucas (wife of George) viewed the rushes daily, but it became clear by the end of filming that the date for delivery of the finished print was too close, so extra editors, Tom Rolf and Mel Shapiro were brought on board to assist.

The shoot-out in the brothel was a particularly complex set piece. For the overhead shot, as the camera slowly tracks out, a hole had to be cut in the ceiling; unfortunately the building was in such an unstable state that when this was done, it started to crack completely and scaffolding had to be erected to stop it falling down! Eventually the camera operator was mounted on a track and had to be pulled round by technicians. There were also limits to the amount of filming which could be done each day, as Foster's daily working hours were limited due to her age (not quite thirteen).

The make-up and special effects needed for the whole shoot-out sequence were co-ordinated by Dick Smith, who had to work in a very confined space. For the shooting off of the hand a false hand was constructed which could be worn by the actor and blown up with a small explosive device. The mafioso's face was fitted with tiny bags of false blood, yanked off with fine, near-invisible thread at the appropriate moment. Even fragments of polysterene cups were used to simulate bits of exploding brain. De Niro wore a skull cap with the mohawk attached to the top and polaroids had to be taken each day to ensure that it looked consistent.

In editing, the main problem for the filmmakers was the ending, which the MPAA (Motion Pictures Association of America) wanted cut if the film were to get anything other than an 'X' certificate. Scorsese and Julia Phillips met with executives from the distributor, Columbia Pictures, who threatened to recut it themselves if Scorsese would not do it. Scorsese, seeing himself as an 'artist', gathered industry friends such as De Palma and Spielberg to support him, but Phillips shrewdly showed the film to influential critics, particularly Pauline Kael, who offered her weighty support. United Artists offered to buy the project from Columbia and release it as an 'X', a category that had done them no harm with *Midnight Cowboy* (1969) and *Last Tango in Paris* (1973). This proved unnecessary, however, as Scorsese agreed to cut a few frames of blood spraying and to desaturate the colour in the shoot-out, thereby toning down the startling and gory red effect, so the film was released with an 'R' rating.

advertising and trailers

The main trailer for the film focuses strongly upon De Niro, his star image from previous performances and the obsessive nature of the character of Travis Bickle. Other actors are mentioned and shown briefly on screen in exchanges with De Niro, but a low key series of images and near-hushed voice-over creates a brooding atmosphere for the potential spectator. The weaponry is shown and the voice-over suggests he is 'looking for a target, getting organised', but there are no images from the final shoot-out which would give too much away.

The poster for the film features Travis, hands in pockets, head down, walking down the street towards the camera, with a porn cinema in the background. The image is given a blue wash, to add to the gloomy effect,

masculine urban alienation

and is accompanied by the tag line: 'On every street in every city there's a
nobody who dreams of being a somebody'. Though there are other figures
in the image, they are far in the background and indistinct, so that the eye
is drawn only to Travis. The bleak impression of masculine urban alienation
is very clear.

Taxi Driver opened in New York on 8 February 1976. It was a great success
critically and commercially, taking $58,000 in its first week in New York and
$12.5 million on general release. For an initial investment of $1.9 million,
this was a very good return.

> I thought at the time we were making a labour of love, that we
> weren't necessarily making a movie that would speak to that many
> people. I was surprised when it had such an acceptance
>
> *Scorsese, Making Taxi Driver, 1998*

audience

The popularity of the film, both at the time of release and subsequently,
does seem to indicate that it strikes a chord in some way, particularly with
young males. De Niro's performance is usually high on the list of what
viewers 'rate' about the film, and as Schrader has suggested, the
loneliness/alienation themes seem to tap in quite strongly to universally
felt emotions. Unofficial websites devoted to *Taxi Driver* give some insight
into its appeal as a 'cult' film; there is an element of the 'forbidden' in this,
particularly in its treatment of violence, but there is also a certain
'alternative' appeal in the style of the film, through the camerawork and
unconventional editing.

critical views

A number of writers have discussed the film in terms of Scorsese's
authorship and the contradictions apparent between his 'world-view' and
that of Schrader. Robin Wood (1988) and Lawrence Friedman (1997) are
notable in this respect. Others, such as Robert Philip Kolker (1988), have
placed the film more in the context of the work of all the 'movie brat'

the hinckley case

directors and the common features across their work. Still others, such as Leighton Grist (1994), have tended to examine the film in its generic context, usually as a film noir.

An important element of many of the reviews of the film at the time of its release was their discussion of violence. Some, like Richard Schickel in *Time* (1976) found the violence 'forced and – coming after so much dreariness – ridiculously pyrotechnical', while others like Judith Crist in *Saturday Review* (1976) described it as 'one of the most revolting outbursts of blood ever to splatter a non-martial arts movie'. However, the violence had its defenders too:

> The violence in this movie is so threatening precisely because it is so cathartic for Travis ... This film ... by drawing us into the vortex, makes us understand the psychic discharge of the quiet boys who go berserk.
>
> *Pauline Kael, New Yorker, 1976*

the hinckley case

Controversy about whether there exists a relationship between on-screen violence and real-life violence is not unusual, and in 1981 it was to surface with particular reference to *Taxi Driver*, when an attempt was made on the life of President Reagan. A suburban loner, John Hinckley, shot the President after stalking not only him but also former president, Jimmy Carter and Jodie Foster.

Hinckley had apparently become obsessed with *Taxi Driver*, having seen it fifteen times and bizarrely claimed his assassination attempt was an act of love for Jodie Foster, who he deluded himself into believing was a prisoner at her college. Fascinated by the fame and publicity associated with assassins, he tape recorded Bickle-like monologues and claimed he was being secretly employed by the government. Like Travis, he stockpiled an arsenal of weapons, drank peach brandy and even photographed himself in a mock suicide pose with a gun to his head. At his trial a lot of the questioning focused upon the possible role of the film and whether Hinckley actually believed himself to be Bickle, but ultimately he was found many structural influences

not guilty by reason of insanity, since he had a major schizophrenic disorder.

Above all, what this case demonstrates is that despite frequent media opinion to the contrary, it is not films which make people into Travis Bickles; Hinckley was lonely and obsessive for several years, indeed, long before he ever saw *Taxi Driver*. The film just gave expression to what he already felt.

genre and influences

The Western, notably *The Searchers* (1956), structures the narrative; film noir determines the mise-en-scène; the horror film spawns the protagonist.

Friedman, 1997, p. 84

Apart from the vast range of moments featuring shots from films which Scorsese had grown up with, which find their way almost subliminally into his films (the glint of a gun in *El Paso*, 1949, in the 'You Talkin' to me' sequence, *The Small Back Room*, 1948, and *The Tales of Hoffmann*, 1950, in the opening shots, shifting points of view from *The Wrong Man*, 1956, framing from *A Bigger Splash*, 1974, the idea of recurring musical motifs from *Murder by Contract*, 1958), *Taxi Driver* has more significant structural influences as indicated by the quotation above.

TAXI DRIVER AS HORROR

The overall idea was to make it like a cross between a Gothic horror and the *New York Daily News*.

Scorsese, 1989, p. 54

The horror film can perhaps be said to have moved from the Transylvanian castles of its early years into suburbia some time in the 1960s. The monster as supernatural being and/or as foreigner (e.g. *Dracula*), tended to shift, from the 1960s, to the monster as a product of the community itself. In the films of Wes Craven, John Carpenter, George Romero and even Alfred Hitchcock, the monster became increasingly located within suburban America, living amongst and rising from the midst of middle-class Americans. Anxiety over the apparent rise of the urban serial killer and a

222.

sense of masculinity under threat in the post-feminist era is often communicated in these fantasies. Travis Bickle can in many ways be seen as such a character – unhinged, the result of America's exploitation of its young men in a faraway war, now back gliding through the streets by night in his cab. Sexually inept and frustrated, by the end of the film his behaviour becomes as monstrous as any of the protagonists of slasher films, like *Hallow'een* (1978) or *Nightmare on Elm Street* (1984).

Several critics have suggested it is close to *Psycho* (1960), with the main difference being that Travis is let loose where Norman Bates is locked up at the end. Both are stories of repressed sexuality returning in monstrous form in an orgy of blood-letting; both are truly modern in their representation of horror.

TAXI DRIVER AS FILM NOIR

Schrader has written about the noir influence as the 'psychotic action and suicidal impulse' of the films of 1949–53:

> The noir hero, seemingly under the weight of ... years of despair, started to go bananas. The psychotic killer, who had in the first period been a subject worthy of study ... now became the active protagonist ... Film noir's final phase was the most aesthetically and sociologically piercing. After ten years of steadily shedding romantic conventions, the later noir films finally got down to the root causes of the period: the loss of public honor, heroic conventions, personal integrity, and, finally, psychic stability. The third phase films were painfully self-aware; they seemed to know they stood at the end of a long tradition based on despair and distintegration.
>
> *Schrader, in Jackson, 1990, pp. 87–9*

Taxi Driver stands in this tradition of 'painful self-awareness' and certainly represents its hero in a similar way. Visually, its use of light and shade is what Grist (1994) has described as 'a successful reworking of noir expressionism, *Taxi Driver* presents a dark, claustrophobic world lit by the glare of garish, symbolic reds and greens' (p. 272).

the city dirt becomes the battleground

The conventions of noir involve reference back to the world of German expressionism where the artist represents the 'complexity of the psyche' by 'selective and creative distortion of the world' to show how the subject sees the world, not how the world objectively is (Eisner, 1973, p. 23–4).

In *Taxi Driver* this is made apparent particularly in the use of anti-realist devices such as the dissolves, overhead shots and the slow motion. These expressionist features, allied to the noir lighting style, the hero's paranoid world view and voice-over, the use of literal and symbolic reflections in this rainy night in the city and even its imagined femme fatale (Betsy) give the film many of the characteristics of noir.

TAXI DRIVER AS A POST-VIETNAM WAR FILM

Like many films of the 1970s and 1980s, *Taxi Driver* can be described as a post-Vietnam War film. Its central character is a former marine, telling the Dispatcher at the cab firm that he had an honourable discharge; he may even have got the job because the interviewer was himself a marine. He dresses in combat fatigues signalling potential or actual violence. Perhaps he is haunted by wartime memories, but unlike other films, such as *Firefox* (1982) or *The Deer Hunter* (1978) there is nothing specific to indicate this. The audience is left to imagine his experiences. Yet driving his cab takes on the same kind of role as fighting in the war, with the dirt of the city as his battleground.

Though the title of the film leaves him as a kind of everyman (there could be lots of these taxi drivers riding around in an alienated state), his combat jacket, desire for the order and ritual of a soldier's life and particularly his commando actions at the end indicate the significance of the war as a contributory factor to his behaviour.

TAXI DRIVER AS WESTERN

What *Taxi Driver* borrows from westerns is more than just Travis having a haircut and Sport's overall appearance. The film is very closely linked to the narrative of John Ford's film *The Searchers* (1956). Scorsese freely talks of this as a western that had always fascinated him; it is even referred to by characters in both *Who's that Knocking on My Door* (1969) and *Mean Streets* (1973).

The protagonist of *The Searchers* is Ethan Edwards (John Wayne). He, like Travis, is a war veteran, this time a confederate. He too is disaffected and still psychologically damaged years after the war. His niece Debbie is the sole survivor, taken by the Indians, following a Comanche raid that massacred his brother's family. Ethan's quest is to rescue Debbie, but he has a further motive, to get Scar, the Comanche chief who kidnapped her. He fears that the kidnapped child will become the violated woman, stigmatized as an Indian consort. As time passes and he searches, it becomes harder to tell whether he will take her home or kill her, seeing her as better off dead than dishonoured.

Taxi Driver is an updated version of *The Searchers*, translated to an urban environment. The lone hero, with his obsessive quest for the young female who does not want to be rescued, murderous intentions and even racism, in both films is like a stranger to the territory, sealed off from society. In Travis's case the cab just emphasises this as he prowls the city by night.

In *The Searchers*, Ethan is in love with Martha, his brother's wife. When she dies, his affections are transferred to her daughter, Debbie. Travis's obsession with Betsy is likewise transferred to Iris, another despoiled child. In both cases these obsessive affections give them the excuse to let their violence have free rein. Scar is scalped by Edwards, Sport is shot by Travis. At the end of each film, the avenging angel goes off again, alone, just as he had arrived, leaving an uneasy feeling for the spectator – Debbie is 'home' but the community is uncomfortable with her return; Iris is 'home' but it all seems hollow.

TAXI DRIVER AND EXISTENTIALISM

While Scorsese's influences are mainly filmic, Schrader's are a mixture of film and literature. His debt to noir has already been mentioned, but he was also particularly fascinated by European and Japanese cinema. He has suggested that the difference between Travis and the European or Japanese counterpart lies in the American's attempts to push his aggression outward, thus killing others, as opposed to the old-world character who turns inward and kills himself.

He also drew heavily on European literary sources, notably existentialist works such as Sartre's *Nausea* (1979), where the hero feels a sickness as a result of modern living, and Dostoevsky's *Notes from the Underground* (1864) in which Dostoevsky's anonymous tormented underground man also lives in a nightmare cityscape, in this case St Petersburg. Scorsese had read the book and felt that Schrader's script came close to capturing its essence. Certainly it finds strong echoes in *Taxi Driver*: 'I am a sick man ... I am a spiteful man', is the underground man's first diary entry in *Notes from the Underground*. 'I believe my liver is diseased', which finds an echo in Travis's hypochondria. Like Travis, the underground man is tormented by repressed desire and fantasies and like Travis he tries to rescue a prostitute.

So the film is essentially a melting pot of literary and cinematic influences without ever becoming totally in thrall to any one of them. From Godard to Bresson, from Ford to Hitchcock, from existentialism to expressionism, this vision of the nightmare city draws upon a whole range of other texts.

bibliography

general film

Altman, Rick, *Film Genre*,
BFI, 1999
Detailed exploration of film genres

Bordwell, David, *Narration in the Fiction Film*, Routledge, 1985
A detailed study of narrative theory and structures

– – –, Staiger, Janet & Thompson, Kristin, *The Classical Hollywood Cinema: Film Style & Mode of Production to 1960*, Routledge, 1985; pbk 1995
An authoritative study of cinema as institution, it covers film style and production

– – – & Thompson, Kristin, *Film Art*, McGraw-Hill, 4th edn, 1993
An introduction to film aesthetics for the non-specialist

Branson, Gill & Stafford, Roy, *The Media Studies Handbook*, Routledge, 1996

Buckland, Warren, *Teach Yourself Film Studies*, Hodder & Stoughton, 1998
Very accessible, it gives an overview of key areas in film studies

Cook, Pam (ed.), *The Cinema Book*, BFI, 1994

Corrigan, Tim, *A Short Guide To Writing About Film*, HarperCollins, 1994
What it says: a practical guide for students

Dyer, Richard, *Stars*, BFI, 1979; pbk Indiana University Press, 1998
A good introduction to the star system

Easthope, Antony, *Classical Film Theory*, Longman, 1993
A clear overview of recent writing about film theory

Hayward, Susan, *Key Concepts in Cinema Studies*, Routledge, 1996

Hill, John & Gibson, Pamela Church (eds), *The Oxford Guide to Film Studies*, Oxford University Press, 1998
Wide-ranging standard guide

Lapsley, Robert & Westlake, Michael, *Film Theory: An Introduction*, Manchester University Press, 1994

Maltby, Richard & Craven, Ian, *Hollywood Cinema*, Blackwell, 1995
A comprehensive work on the Hollywood industry and its products

Mulvey, Laura, 'Visual Pleasure and Narrative Cinema' (1974), in *Visual and Other Pleasures*, Indiana University Press, Bloomington, 1989
The classic analysis of 'the look' and 'the male gaze' in Hollywood cinema. Also available in numerous other edited collections

Nelmes, Jill (ed.), *Introduction to Film Studies*, Routledge, 1996
Deals with several national cinemas and key concepts in film study

Nowell-Smith, Geoffrey (ed.), *The Oxford History of World Cinema*, Oxford University Press, 1996
Hugely detailed and wide-ranging with many features on 'stars'

general film

Thomson, David, *A Biographical Dictionary of the Cinema*, Secker & Warburg, 1975
Unashamedly driven by personal taste, but often stimulating

Truffaut, François, *Hitchcock*, Simon & Schuster, 1966, rev. edn, Touchstone, 1985
Landmark extended interview

Turner, Graeme, *Film as Social Practice*, 2nd edn, Routledge, 1993
Chapter four, 'Film Narrative', discusses structuralist theories of narrative

Wollen, Peter, *Signs and Meaning in the Cinema*, Viking, 1972
An important study in semiology

Readers should also explore the many relevant websites and journals. *Film Education* and *Sight and Sound* are standard reading.

Valuable websites include:

The Internet Movie Database at http://uk.imdb.com

Screensite at http://www.tcf.ua.edu/screensite/contents.html

The Media and Communications Site at the University of Aberystwyth at http://www.aber.ac.uk/~dgc/welcome.html

There are obviously many other university and studio websites which are worth exploring in relation to film studies.

taxi driver

Biskind, Peter, *Easy Riders, Raging Bulls*, Bloomsbury, 1998
An exposé of the inside of the film industry in the 1970s

Boyd, David, 'Prisoner of the Night', *Film Heritage*, vol.12, no.2, 1976–7

Brottman, Mikita, 'Taxi Driver', in Jack Hunter (ed.), *Robert De Niro: Movie Top Ten*, Creation Books, 1999
An overview of ten of De Niro's film roles, including four of his collaborations with Scorsese

Crist, Judith, 'Taxi Driver', *Saturday Review*, 1 March 1976

Dostoevsky, Fyodor, *Notes from the Underground*, 1864
One of the literary influences upon Schrader's screenplay

Eisner, Lotte, *The Haunted Screen*, University of California Press, 1973

A key work on German expressionist cinema

Flatley, Guy, 'Martin Scorsese's Gamble', in Peter Brunette (ed.), *Martin Scorsese Interviews*, University of Mississippi, 1999
Interviews taken from various points in Scorsese's career

Friedman, Lawrence S., *The Cinema of Martin Scorsese*, Roundhouse, Oxford, 1997
Detailed analysis of all of Scorsese's films up to *Casino* (1995)

Grist, Leighton, 'Moving Targets and Black Widows – Film Noir in Modern Hollywood', in Ian Cameron (ed.), *The Movie Book of Film Noir*, Studio Vista, 1994
A set of essays analysing the genre; this chapter includes some

consideration of modern 'neo-noir' films such as *Taxi Driver*

Gross, Larry, 'Film Apres Noir', *Film Comment*, vol.12 no.4, 1976

Hinckley, Jack and Jo Ann, with Sherrill, Elizabeth, **Breaking Points**, Chosen Books, Grand Rapids, 1985
The parents of John Hinckley analyse their son's behaviour

Jacobs, Diane, **Hollywood Renaissance**, Delta, New York, 1980
Looks at the early work of Scorsese and other new filmmakers of the late 1960s and 1970s

Kael, Pauline, 'Underground Man', *The New Yorker*, 9 February 1976

Kelly, Mary Pat, **Martin Scorsese: The First Decade**, Redgrave, New York, 1980
A quirky collection of interviews and reviews, includes some interesting storyboard material

Kolker, Robert Philip, **A Cinema of Loneliness**, 2nd edition, OUP, 1988
A detailed study of the work of several American directors of the 1970s and 1980s

Kroll, Jack, 'Taxi Driver', *Newsweek*, 1 March 1976

Pye, Michael, and Miles, Lynda, **The Movie Brats**, New York, 1979
Looks at the new generation of directors which emerged from film school in the late 60s and their influence on Hollywood

Pirie, David, 'Taxi Driver', *Time Out*, 1976, reprinted in Tom Milne, *Time Out Film Guide*, 1982

Sartre, Jean-Paul, **Nausea**, (translator: Robert Baldick), Penguin, 1979
Existentialist novel, an influence upon Schrader's screenplay

Schickel, Richard, 'Taxi Driver', *Time*, 16 February 1976

Schrader, Paul, **Taxi Driver**, Faber, 1990
The screenplay of the film

Schrader, Paul, **Schrader on Schrader**, Kevin Jackson (ed.), Faber, London, 1990
Interviews with the writer/director about his work

Scorsese, Martin, **Scorsese on Scorsese**, David Thomson and Ian Christie (eds), Faber, London, 1989
The definitive interviews

Sharrett, Christopher, **Crisis Cinema: The Apocalyptic idea in Postmodern American Film**, Washington DC, 1993

Taubin, Amy, **Taxi Driver**, BFI Film Classics, London, 2000

Wood, Robin, **Hollywood from Vietnam to Reagan**, Columbia University Press, 1986
A lively collection of essays

Other source material cited

Scene by Scene with Martin Scorsese BBC2, 1998

Scene by Scene with Paul Schrader, BBC2, 1998

Making Taxi Driver (dir. Laurent Bouzereau 1998) available on the DVD release of the film, *Taxi Driver: Collector's Edition* 1999 Columbia Pictures

Taxi Driver, original soundtrack CD, Arista records remastered extended play 1998

Unpublished essays can be found on the internet movie database: www.imdb.com
an excellent resource for all kinds of information about films

Various unofficial websites devoted to the film

filmography

Films directed by Martin Scorsese

The Big Shave (short, 1967)

Who's that Knocking at My Door? (1969)

Boxcar Bertha (1972)

Mean Streets (1973)

Italianamerican (1974)

Alice Doesn't Live Here Anymore (1974)

Taxi Driver (1976)

New York, New York (1977)

The Last Waltz (1978)

American Boy (1978)

Raging Bull (1980)

The King of Comedy (1982)

After Hours (1985)

The Color of Money (1986)

The Last Temptation of Christ (1988)

GoodFellas (1990)

Cape Fear (1991)

The Age of Innocence (1993)

Casino (1995)

Kundun (1997)

Bringing out the Dead (1999)

Robert De Niro Filmography

Greetings (De Palma USA 1968)

Sam's Song (Leondopolous USA 1969)

The Wedding Party (De Palma USA 1969)

Bloody Mama (Corman USA 1970)

Hi, Mom! (De Palma USA 1970)

Born To Win (Passer USA 1971)

The Gang That Couldn't Shoot Straight (Goldstone USA 1971)

Jennifer On My Mind (Black USA 1971)

Bang The Drum Slowly (Hancock USA 1973)

Mean Streets (Scorsese USA 1973)

The Godfather: Part II (Coppola USA 1974)

1900 (Bertolucci Italy 1976)

Taxi Driver (Scorsese USA 1976)

The Last Tycoon (Kazan USA 1976)

New York, New York (Scorsese USA 1977)

The Deer Hunter (Cimino USA 1978)

Raging Bull (Scorsese USA 1980)

True Confessions (Grosbard USA 1981)

The King of Comedy (Scorsese USA 1983)

Falling In Love (Grosbard USA 1984)

Once Upon A Time In America (Leone USA 1984)

Brazil (Gilliam USA 1985)

The Mission (Joffe USA 1986)

The Untouchables (De Palma USA 1987)

Angel Heart (Parker USA 1987)

Midnight Run (Brest USA 1988)

Jacknife (Hugh-Jones USA 1989)

We're No Angels (Jordan USA 1989)

GoodFellas (Scorsese USA 1990)

Stanley & Iris (Ritt USA 1990)

Awakenings (Marshall USA 1990)

Backdraft (Howard USA 1991)

Guilty By Suspicion (Winkler USA 1991)

Cape Fear (Scorsese USA 1991)

Mistress (Primus USA 1992)

Night And The City (Winkler USA 1992)

This Boy's Life (Caton-Jones USA 1993)

Mad Dog And Glory (McNaughton USA 1993)

filmography

A Bronx Tale (De Niro USA 1993)

Mary Shelley's Frankenstein (Branagh USA 1994)

Heat (Mann USA 1995)

Casino (Scorsese USA 1995)

Marvin's Room (Zaks USA 1996)

Sleepers (Levinson USA 1996)

The Fan (Scott USA 1996)

Jackie Brown (Tarantino USA 1997)

Wag The Dog (Levinson USA 1997)

Copland (Mangold USA 1997)

Great Expectations (Cuaron USA 1998)

Ronin (Frankenheimer USA 1998)

Flawless (Schumacher USA 1999)

Analyze This (Ramis USA 1999)

15 Minutes (Discenzo, USA 2000)

The Adventures of Rocky and Bullwinkle (McAnuff USA 2000)

Films mentioned in Narrative and Form

Born on the Fourth of July (Stone USA 1990)

Citizen Kane (Welles USA 1941)

Deux ou Trois Choses que Je Sais d'Elle / Two or Three Things I Know About Her (Godard France 1967)

Journal d'un Cure de Campagne / Diary of a Country Priest (Bresson France 1950)

Enter the Dragon (Clouse USA/Hong Kong 1973)

A Fistful of Dollars (Leone, Italy/Germany/Spain 1964)

King Kong (Cooper/ Schoedsack 1933)

Mishima (Schrader USA/Japan 1985)

Peeping Tom (Powell UK 1960)

Psycho (Hitchcock USA 1960)

Les Quatre Cents Coups / The 400 Blows (Truffaut France 1959)

Return of the Dragon (Chiang Hong Kong 1972)

The Searchers (Ford USA 1956)

Seven (Fincher USA 1995)

The Small Back Room (Powell/Pressburger UK 1948)

The Tales of Hoffmann (Powell/Pressburger UK 1951)

The Texas Chainsaw Massacre (Hooper USA 1974)

The Wild Bunch (Peckinpah USA 1969)

Films Mentioned in Contexts

A Bigger Splash (Hazan UK 1974)

A Nightmare on Elm Street (Craven USA 1984)

The Deer Hunter (Cimino USA 1978)

El Paso (Foster USA 1949)

Firefox (Eastwood USA 1982)

Halloween (Carpenter USA 1978)

Murder By Contract (Lerner USA 1958)

The Wrong Man (Hitchcock USA 1956)

cinematic terms

auteur a French word meaning the 'author' of the film. Usually, this is taken to be the director, though debates over authorship indicate the problems with simply ascribing everything about the film to one person

bankable term applied to a star, a director or even a screenwriter, whose past work has been commercially successful, leading to the assumption that future projects with his/her name attached will be a box office success

blockbuster a high budget film designed to appeal to a mass audience

body double an actor who stands in for the principal actor, often for nude or sex scenes, not involving their face appearing on camera

catharsis bringing pent-up emotions to the surface and thus getting rid of their effects. According to the Greek philosopher, Aristotle, plays can have this effect on the audience by playing out the spectator's repressed feelings. The same theory might be applied to films

cineastes people who are very keen and frequent film-watchers and who spend a lot of time discussing films; cinema experts

cineliteracy having a clear understanding of the rules or grammar of film making through a detailed knowledge of films, probably by having watched and studied many of them

cinematographer/director of photography the leader of the photography unit on a film. Supervises all camera operation and lighting and will make decisions in collaboration with the director on how each scene will be lit and filmed

continuity system/editing the dominant system of editing developed by Hollywood, which is used to maintain continuous narrative action, to enable the audience to be clear about what is happening. Such editing has to be 'invisible', or at least not to draw attention to itself *as* editing, so that the audience focuses upon the action rather than the camerawork or editing

diegetic sound any sound in the film presented as if it comes from a source within the film's world

diegesis the world of the film's story

director the person in creative control of the film, in charge of all the planning, shooting and post-production processes

dissolve transition from one shot to another in which as one shot is faded out, the next is simultaneously faded in

documentary realism a style of film making which, while retaining a fictional narrative, gives the look of a documentary

dolly a camera support with wheels, used for tracking shots

editor selects and joins together pieces of footage to make the film

existentialism a term denying objective universal values and holding that a person must create values for him/ herself through action and by living each moment to the full

expressionism a movement in the arts, particularly apparent in 1920s Germany, which involved moving away from the outer life into exploring the inner. In cinema, this often took the form of exaggerated sets and lighting representing how the character saw the world rather than how the world objectively was

film noir a French term which translates as 'dark film', applied to a type of Hollywood film, mainly made in the 1940s and 1950s, characterised by low-key lighting and bleak mood, usually set in the city and featuring criminal activity

cinematic terms

French New Wave a movement in film in the late 1950s and 1960s, notably featuring the work of Francois Truffaut and Jean-Luc Godard, which both celebrated Hollywood genre films in its style and broke' many of the rules of continuity editing in its form of storytelling

Hollywood studio system the factory-based method by which films were made in the period from about 1930 to 1960, where personnel were contracted to particular studios, such as MGM or Warner Brothers, and (on the whole) assigned projects to make into films rather than choosing or initiating their own projects, as in the 1970s

jump cut a cut which appears to be an interruption of a single shot (i.e. a mistake). It may involve a repetition of an action (as in the 'You talkin' to me' sequence)

method actor a style of acting which involves the actor immersing him/herself in the role, as if 'living' the part

mise-en-scène everything which is placed in front of the camera, such as sets, props, lighting, costume and human figures

motif a significant element which is repeated in the film

narrative the overall form into which the events of the film are organised.

niche audience a small segment of the audience at whom a specific film might be targeted

non-diegetic sound a sound coming from a source outside the film's world (such as the music on the soundtrack)

pan sideways movement of the camera

point-of-view shot (POV) a shot taken with the camera as if through the eyes of a character

post-production any work done on the film after shooting, such as editing and dubbing sound

producer the person who holds the 'purse strings' for the film, in charge of seeing that the film comes in on time and on budget

protagonist the central character whose actions drive the narrative forward

reverse shot a shot taken from the opposite position to the previous shot, e.g. first shot shows someone looking, second (reverse) shows what they are looking at

rushes the raw footage shot and developed, often available for screening the day after it has been filmed

screenplay the written text for a film, with dialogue and some directions/ descriptions of character and setting

screenwriter writer of the screenplay

star vehicle a film built around the image of a star and usually sold to audiences on that basis

storyboard a series of drawings to represent a sequence of shots, planned out in advance of shooting and used as a guide for the filmmakers

temporal use of time in the film

tilt a vertical movement of the camera

track a movement of the camera itself backward or forward. The camera will usually be mounted on a dolly

verité literally 'truth'; in cinema giving an apparently direct version of reality

zip pan a fast sideways movement of the camera which gives a blurred effect. Sometimes used instead of a cut to show a sudden movement or reaction of shock

zoom a movement in or out by the lens during a shot

credits

director
Martin Scorsese

screenplay
Paul Schrader

producers
Michael Phillips, Julia Phillips

cinematography
Michael Chapman

editors
Marcia Lucas, Tom Rolf,
Melvin Shapiro

visual consultant
David Nichols

special effects
Dick Smith

music
Bernard Herrmann

associate producer
Philip Goldfarb

assistant director
Charles Rosen

camera operator
Fred Schuler

assistant editors
George Trivogoff, William Weber

music editor
Shinichi Yamazaki

costume designer
Ruth Morley

special effects
Tony Parmelee

second unit camera
Michael Zingale

assistant director
Peter R. Scoppa

running time
113 min

distributor
Columbia Pictures

cast
Wizard – Peter Boyle
Tom – Albert Brooks
Travis Bickle – Robert De Niro
Iris – Jodie Foster
Charles Palantine – Leonard Harris
Sport – Harvey Keitel
Dough-Boy – Harry Northup
Andy, gun salesman –
Steven Prince
Betsy – Cybill Shepherd